Introduction

I0464865

Welcome to the Green Book — a comprehensive guide for financial institutions that receive ACH payments from the Federal government.

Today, the vast majority of Federal payments are made via the ACH. With very few exceptions, Federal government ACH transactions continue to be subject to the same rules as private industry ACH payments. As a result, the Green Book continues to get smaller in size and is designed to deal primarily with exceptions or issues unique to Federal government operations.

Federal agency contact information is included and, since so much information is available via the Internet, web site addresses are included where appropriate. The Green Book continues to be available on the Internet at www.fms.treas.gov/greenbook and chapters can be printed as Portable Display Format (PDF) documents. We no longer print and mail hard copies. So, we encourage you to visit the web site for updates and news relevant to Federal government ACH transactions.

The ACH regulation, 31 CFR 210, provides the basis for most of the information contained in the Green Book. However, there are other regulations that impact Federal government ACH payments. The following table summarizes these regulations;

Regulation	Governs
31 CFR Part 210	Federal Government Participation in the Automated Clearing House
31 CFR Part 208	Management of Federal Agency Disbursements
31 CFR Part 370	Electronic Transactions and Funds Transfers Relating to United States Securities

We still occasionally get asked, "Why green?" It is really simple. The first publication issued in 1975 dealing with the Direct Deposit of Federal government payments, when the ACH network was in its infancy, had a green cover. More than 30 years later, the world of Federal government payments has changed, but the Green Book is still green! We hope you incorporate the Green Book into your daily operations and visit us frequently.

Department of the Treasury
Bueau of the Fiscal Service
April 2013

1 Enrollment for Federal Payments

Overview

Financial Institutions can play a key role in assisting recipients of federal payments to enroll in Direct Deposit with their paying agency. This chapter is a guide to the various enrollment methods available for both consumer and corporate recipients. Institutions who choose to process their own enrollments electronically may do so through the Automated Clearing House (ACH) system. Through the use of the ENR code in the ACH system, Financial institutions expedite the processing and transfer of the enrollment information to governmental paying agencies. There are several enrollment options:

1. Enroll customers in lobby, batch and submit ENR enrollments through ACH from the Financial institution

2. Financial Institution can enroll on the *Go Direct*® website to enter enrollments for customers

3. Financial Institution can call the *Go Direct* 800 number for immediate enrollment of customers

4. Enrollment using FMS form 1200 for SSA/SSI, RRB, and OPM payments and Direct Deposit Sign Up Form SF 1199A for other Federal payments, or the ACH Vendor/Miscellaneous Payment Enrollment Form SF 3881 for corporate vendor payments

Errors in the Direct Deposit enrollment process are the primary cause of misdirected payments. Financial institutions will be held liable for providing incorrect enrollment information and should, therefore, carefully review all Direct Deposit enrollment procedures.

In this Chapter...

A: Automated Enrollment (ENR)

Automated enrollment is a convenient method for financial institutions to use the Automated Clearing House (ACH) network to transmit Direct Deposit enrollment information directly to Federal agencies for benefit payments. An ENR entry is a non-dollar entry sent through the ACH by any Receiving Depository Financial Institution (RDFI) to a Federal government agency participating in the ENR program

ENR is the enrollment method preferred by Federal benefit agencies. The ENR reduces errors in the enrollment process and allows Direct Deposit payments to begin sooner than paper enrollment methods.

An ENR should be used when the recipient is executing a new authorization. This may represent a first-time sign-up for Direct Deposit or a change in financial institutions. The ENR should not be used for changes to existing Direct Deposit enrollments. To change financial institution data for an existing Direct Deposit enrollment, you must use a Notification of Change (NOC). An NOC represents a correction in account information within the existing authorization. (Refer to Chapter 6 for more information on NOCs.)

Enrollments received and accepted by the paying agency at least 10 business days prior to the customer's next scheduled payment date will generally allow the recipient's next month's payment by Direct Deposit.

Note: Please refer to your current NACHA ACH Rules for formats and instructions.

Go Direct Online Enrollment Option for Financial Institutions

In addition to the Automated ENR option, Financial Institutions can also choose to take advantage of enrollment via the Go Direct website, *www.GoDirect.org*. The Go Direct campaign was a national marketing and public education campaign sponsored by the U.S. Treasury and the Federal Reserve that increased the use of Direct Deposit for Federal benefit check recipients. Although the Go Direct campaign has officially concluded, Financial Institutions can continue to utilize the enrollment website. Financial Institutions can create a secure UserID/password (profile) that will allow for repeated enrollments for customers to be completed very easily. Please review the Go Direct User Guide for Financial Institutions.
(*https://www.godirect.gov/SignUp/Org/UserGuide/Go%20Direct%20User%20Guide%20FI.pdf*)

Enrollments submitted through the Go Direct enrollment site will be verified and submitted to the respective paying agencies by the U.S. Treasury Electronic Payment Solutions Center. The U.S. Treasury Electronic Payment Solutions Center is housed and operated in a secure Federal Reserve facility. Financial Institution customers who are enrolled through the web site and successfully verified against paying agency records will receive a Confirmation Notice, by USPS, from the U.S. Treasury Electronic Payment Solutions Center once the enrollment is ready to be transmitted to their paying agency. Financial Institution customers whose enrollments can not be verified or processed will be contacted by the U.S. Treasury Electronic Payment Solutions Center via letter delivered by USPS.

All reject or return item processing for these items is handled by the Research Division of the Processing Center. Financial institutions electing to submit enrollments electronically through Go Direct are relieved of the obligation of processing ENR return items (refer to: Appendix - Enrollments - Return Items)

SSA Payment Cycling

Since June 1997, the payment date for newly enrolled Social Security beneficiaries is either the second, third, or fourth Wednesday of the month. These additional payment days alleviate the workload peaks for SSA, FMS, and the financial and business communities. However, in instances where the beneficiary receives both SSA and SSI payments, the payments are issued on the standard 1st and 3rd schedule.

B: Simplified Enrollment

There are a variety of ways for Federal payment recipients to enroll for Direct Deposit without visiting a financial institution.

Telephone Enrollment

Federal benefit recipients can be enrolled by calling the U.S. Treasury Electronic Payment Solutions Center at 1-800-333-1795 (English) / 1-800-333-1792 (Spanish), or by visiting www. GoDirect.org, or by completing FMS Form 1200. The U.S. Treasury Electronic Payment Solutions Center hours of operation are 8:00 am - 8:00 pm ET, Monday through Friday excluding Federal holidays.

Financial institution representatives (i.e. new accounts, customer service, etc) can also assist their customers (recipient's) who wish to enroll by phone. However, when doing so, the benefit recipient - or their representative - must be present when the phone call is made. U.S. Treasury Electronic Payment Solutions Center personnel will ask to speak to the recipient or their representative and obtain approval for the 3rd party banking representative to provide their enrollment information. Financial institutions that elect to capture enrollment information on paper or through other means and process after hours or in a back-office environment may not use U.S. Treasury Electronic Payment Solutions Center telephone enrollment on behalf of their customer.

Paper Form Enrollment

Recipients who elect to complete FMS paper form 1200 should complete it on their own or with the assistance of a Financial Institution representative (for the RTN and account number) and mail to:

> U.S. Treasury Electronic Payment Solutions Center
> U.S. Department of the Treasury
> P.O. Box 650527
> Dallas, Texas 75265-0527

The table below shows the Simplified Enrollment procedures for specific payment types.

Enrollment Methods for Specific Payments

Payment Type	Recipient
Allotments Federal Salary Federal Employment-Related Payments (i.e., Travel Reimbursement, Uniform Allowance, etc.)	Completes an approved form at his/her Federal agency personnel office (e.g. , FMS Form 2231, *FastStart* Direct Deposit). Some Federal employees are able to make changes to Direct Deposit information via telephone using *Employee Express*. Recipients should contact their servicing personnel office for more information.
IRS Tax Refunds	Completes the financial institution information section of the IRS Form 1040 during tax preparation. For paper filing completes a U.S. Individual Income Tax Declaration (IRS Form 8453). For electronic filing via IRS *e-file* completes an 8453-OL. Recipients should contact the IRS at **1-800-829-1040** or visit *www.irs.gov* for more details.
Railroad Retirement Board (RRB)	Financial Institutions can enroll their customers and/or recipients can enroll individually by calling **1-800-333-1795** (English) / **1-800-333-1792** (Spanish), or by visiting *www.GoDirect.org*, or by completing FMS Form 1200. The U.S. Treasury Electronic Payment Solutions Center hours of operation are 8:00 am - 8:00 pm ET, Monday through Friday, excluding Federal Holidays. Additionally, Financial Institutions and/or recipients can contact RRB's toll-free telephone number at **1-877-772-5772**.
Social Security (SSA) and Supplemental Security Income (SSI)	Financial Institutions can enroll their customers and/or recipients can enroll individually by calling **1-800-333-1795** (English) / **1-800-333-1792** (Spanish), or by visiting *www.GoDirect.org*, or by completing FMS Form 1200. The U.S. Treasury Electronic Payment Solutions Center hours of operation are 8:00 am - 8:00 pm ET, Monday through Friday, excluding Federal Holidays. Additionally, Financial Institutions and/or recipients can enroll by contacting the SSA at **1-800-SSA-1213 (1-800-772-1213)**.

Simplified Enrollment Methods (continued)

Payment Type	Recipient
Office of Personnel Management (OPM) Form *Note: OPM does not allow ENR enrollments for representative payees.*	Financial Institutions can enroll their customers and/or recipients can enroll individually by calling **1-800-333-1795** (English) / **1-800-333-1792** (Spanish), or by visiting *www.GoDirect.org*, or by completing FMS Form 1200. The U.S. Treasury Electronic Payment Solutions Center hours of operation are 8:00 am - 8:00 pm ET, Monday through Friday, excluding Federal Holidays. Additionally, Financial Institutions and/or recipients can call OPM at **1-888-767-6738** or (202) 606-0500 in the Washington, DC area or visit *www.opm.gov/retire* for details.
Bureau of the Fiscal Service *TreasuryDirect*	Enrolls automatically when he/she establishes a *TreasuryDirect* account for purchasing Treasury bills, notes, and bonds. Allows for the Direct Deposit of principal and interest payments. Investors use Form PD F 5182, New Account Request, to establish a *TreasuryDirect* account and to provide Direct Deposit information. Investors use Form PD F 5178, Transaction Request, to change Direct Deposit information. Recipients should contact a designated *TreasuryDirect* Servicing Office or *visit www. treasurydirect.gov* for forms and other information.
Veterans Compensation and Pension *Note: VA does not allow ENR enrollments for representative payees.*	Financial Institutions can enroll their customers and/or recipients can enroll individually by calling **1-800-333-1795** (English) / **1-800-333-1792** (Spanish), or by visiting *www.GoDirect.org*, or by completing FMS Form 1200. The U.S. Treasury Electronic Payment Solutions Center hours of operation are 8:00 am - 8:00 pm ET, Monday through Friday, excluding Federal Holidays. Recipients can also contact the VA National Direct Deposit EFT line at **1-800-827-1000** or visit *www.vba. gov/ro/muskogee* for further details.
Veterans Education *Note: VA does not allow ENR enrollments for representative payees.*	Enrolls at the same time he/she applies for benefits at the VA or at any time after he/she begins receiving benefits. Recipients already receiving benefits should contact the VA Education Direct Deposit EFT line at **1-888-442-4551**.

Simplified Enrollment Methods (continued)

Payment Type	Recipient
Veterans Life Insurance *Note: OPM does not allow ENR enrollments for representative payees.*	Enrolls at the same time he/she applies for benefits at the VA or at any time after he/she begins receiving benefits. Recipients should contact the VA Insurance office at **1-800-669-8477** or visit *www.insurance.va.gov* for further details.

Allotments, Federal Salary, and Federal Employment Related Payments

Recipients who are current Federal employees complete an approved form at their agency personnel office, or for military members, servicing pay office. This form may be an SF 1199A or an FMS Form 2231 (*FastStart* Direct Deposit Sign Up) or a similar form used by the employee's agency. The Direct Deposit payments may be for Federal salaries, allotments, or for employment related payments for travel reimbursement or uniform allowance. It is not necessary for the Federal employee to bring the form to the financial institution for verification of the banking information. However, some may do so if unfamiliar with the account number or routing number.

When Should Direct Deposit Begin Once it Has Been Initiated?

Use the table below to determine when Direct Deposit should begin once the enrollment form is forwarded to the Federal agency.

IF the payment type is...	THEN Direct Deposit should begin within...
Federal Salary Military civilian pay Military active duty Allotments	2-3 pay periods
Recurring benefit Military retirement/annuity	60-90 days

Details of Each Payment Type

IRS Tax Refunds

The Internal Revenue Service (IRS) offers the Direct Deposit of IRS Form 1040 tax refunds for both paper and electronically filed returns.

For IRS Form 1040 paper returns, taxpayers receiving refunds and electing Direct Deposit simply complete the financial institution information section of the form and mail the form to the IRS.

For electronically filed returns using an authorized IRS *e-file* provider, the taxpayer will complete a U.S. Individual Income Tax Declaration for Electronic Filing (IRS Form 8453) for refunds by Direct Deposit. This form authorizes the tax preparer to transmit the return and allows the choice of having the refund deposited into a checking or savings account.

Taxpayers preparing returns on a personal computer using commercial tax preparation software or the IRS Free Online Filing and transmitting the information via modem to the IRS complete Form 8453-OL, U.S. Individual Income Tax Declaration for On-Line Filing. This form allows the taxpayer to choose Direct Deposit for the refund. The financial institution will not receive copies of these forms.

The financial institution should be aware of the following:

1. Enrollment in Direct Deposit for income tax refunds is not a permanent election by the taxpayer. Taxpayers must elect Direct Deposit each filing year.

2. Payments must be returned when they cannot be properly posted by the financial institution. NOCs cannot be used to correct any information. In the instance where a Direct Deposit IRS tax refund is unpostable and returned, taxpayers will receive a check in place of a Direct Deposit payment.

3. The financial institution's responsibility is to post the Direct Deposit payment to the account indicated on the ACH record. As long as the financial institution posts the payment to the account to the account indicated, it has met its responsibility. If the funds are posted to a valid account that turns out to be the wrong account, the financial institution is not liable to the Government for the return of the funds. If the taxpayer or the taxpayer's agent gave the incorrect account information, neither FMS nor the IRS will assist the taxpayer with recovering the funds, and the taxpayer is free to pursue civil action. If, however, the IRS made the error, it will make the taxpayer whole.

For further information, contact the IRS at **1-800-829-1040**; contact the local IRS District Office, or visit *www.irs.gov*.

For IRS tax refund status, the recipient should call the IRS automated refund service at **1-800-829-4477**. (Recipients must supply the Social Security Number, filing status, and amount of the refund.)

Railroad Retirement Board

Financial Institutions can enroll their customers and/or recipients can enroll individually by:

1. Calling **1-800-333-1795** (English) / **1-800-333-1792** (Spanish), or by visiting *www.GoDirect.org*, or by completing FMS Form 1200 The call center hours of operation are 8:00 am - 8:00 pm ET, Monday through Friday, excluding Federal Holidays, or

2. Calling the Railroad Retirement Board at **1-877-772-5772**.

3. Sending a written request to enroll in Direct Deposit to the local Railroad Retirement Board field office. The letter should include the recipient's name and the following:
> A: Account Number
> B: Account type (checking or savings)
> C: Routing number of the financial institution used to receive the ACH items.

Social Security Administration

Financial Institutions can enroll their customers and/or recipients can enroll individually by calling **1-800-333-1795** (English) / **1-800-333-1792** (Spanish), or by visiting *www.GoDirect.org*, or by completing FMS Form 1200 The call center hours of operation are 8:00 am - 8:00 pm ET, Monday through Friday, excluding Federal Holidays.

Additionally, recipients already receiving Social Security and Supplemental Security Income benefits by check may enroll in Direct Deposit by calling the telephone number listed for Social Security in the local telephone book, or **1-800-SSA-1213 (1-800-772-1213)**.

SSA's toll-free telephone service is available from 7:00 am to 7:00 pm Eastern time, Monday through Friday. Due to the high volume of calls, the best times to telephone are in the early morning and during the latter parts of the week and month.

The financial institution may make the call on behalf of the recipient and may provide the enrollment information; however, SSA will request to speak to the recipient to verify his/her identity.

Office of Personnel Management

Financial Institutions can enroll their customers and/or recipients can enroll individually by calling **1-800-333-1795** (English) / **1-800-333-1792** (Spanish), or by visiting *www.GoDirect.org*, or by completing FMS Form 1200 The call center hours of operation are 8:00 am - 8:00 pm ET, Monday through Friday, excluding Federal Holidays.

Additionally, new retirees, annuitants, and survivor annuitants may enroll in Direct Deposit by calling the toll-free customer service number at **1-888-767-6378**. Those in the Washington, DC area are encouraged to call **(202) 606-0500**. Recipients may also visit *www. opm.gov/retire* for instructions on how to change their payment address on-line.

Note: The Office of Personnel Management does not allow ENR enrollments for representative payees.

TreasuryDirect (Bureau of the Fiscal Service)

TreasuryDirect is a book-entry securities system in which investors' accounts of book-entry Treasury marketable securities are maintained. *TreasuryDirect* is designed for investors who purchase Treasury securities and intend to hold them until maturity. Investors can establish a *TreasuryDirect* account and hold all their bills, notes, and bonds in one *TreasuryDirect* account showing the same ownership for all their securities or they can establish multiple accounts reflecting different ownership. Investors will receive a *TreasuryDirect* Statement of Account when they open a new account, when the par amount changes, upon request, or if they have not received one during the calendar year.

TreasuryDirect principal and interest payments are made electronically by Direct Deposit to a checking or savings account at a financial institution designated by the investor. When establishing a *TreasuryDirect* account, investors will complete Form PD F 5182, New Account Request, and will include Direct Deposit information. Investors are not required to fill out an SF 1199A. Investors can also establish an account when they complete Form PD F 5381, Treasury Bill, Note & Bond Tender to purchase a security. Investors use Form PD F 5178, Transaction Request, to change Direct Deposit information for the *TreasuryDirect* account. Financial institutions may be asked by customers to furnish the account number, routing transit number, account type, and/or the financial institution's name. The investor should contact a designated *TreasuryDirect* Servicing Office or visit *www.treasurydirect.gov* for forms and other information.

Simplified Enrollment for Series H/HH Savings Bond Interest Payments (Bureau of the Fiscal Service)

Series H/HH savings bonds are current income securities that pay interest semiannually. Interest on bonds issued since October 1989 to the present must be paid by Direct Deposit. Unless a recipient claims that it will cause a hardship, interest on bonds issued prior to October 1989 must also be paid by Direct Deposit.

To enroll in Direct Deposit or to change their enrollment, recipients may:

1. Download PD F 5396 from *www.savingsbonds.gov*, complete and mail the form as instructed, or

2. Send a letter to the Current Income Bond Branch, Bureau of the Fiscal Service, Parkersburg, WV 26106-2186. The letter should include the following:
     A. Recipient's name

    B. Social Security number
    C. Account number
    D. Account type (checking or savings)
    E. Routing number of the financial institution

Department of Veterans Affairs Direct Deposit

Veterans Compensation and Pension and Vocational Rehabilitation & Employment recipients already receiving benefits may enroll in Direct Deposit by calling **1-800-827-1000**. Compensation and Pension Beneficiaries may also enroll in Direct Deposit through VA's eBenefits self-service portal (*www.ebenefits.va.gov*)

VA Education recipients already receiving benefits may enroll in Direct Deposit by calling **1-888-442-4551**.

New VA benefits recipients should provide Direct Deposit information at the time of application.

Recipients of VA benefits may also enroll by submitting VA Form 24-0296 (Direct Deposit Enrollment) and mailing it to the Station of Jurisdiction over the claim. To locate the Station of Jurisdiction over the claim, visit *http://www.benefits.va.gov/benefits/offices.asp*.

Veterans Life Insurance recipients may enroll in Direct Deposit by calling **1-800-669-8477**. A Direct Deposit enrollment form and further details are also available by visiting *www.insurance.va.gov* or by writing to:

VAROIC - DD
P.O. Box 7208
Philadelphia, PA 19101-7208

New recipients should provide Direct Deposit information at the time of application.

Note: The Department of Veterans Affairs does not allow ENR enrollments for representative payees.

C: Paper Enrollment Methods

FMS Form 1200

The table below identifies those agencies and payment types where the FMS Form 1200 should be used for paper enrollment:

Agency / Payment Type	Recipient
Social Security Administration • Social Security • Supplemental Security Income	Recipients should complete FMS Form 1200 and send completed form to: U.S. Treasury Electronic Payment Solutions Center U.S. Department of Treasury P.O. Box 650527 Dallas, TX 75265-0527

Agency / Payment Type	Recipient
Office of Personnel Management • Annuity • Retirement Annuity or Survivor Annuity	Recipients should complete FMS Form 1200 and send completed form to: U.S. Treasury Electronic Payment Solutions Center U.S. Department of Treasury P.O. Box 650527 Dallas, TX 75265-0527
Railroad Retirement Board • Railroad Retirement Annuity Benefit • Railroad Retirement Unemployment / Sickness	Recipients should complete FMS Form 1200 and send completed form to: U.S. Treasury Electronic Payment Solutions Center U.S. Department of Treasury P.O. Box 650527 Dallas, TX 75265-0527

Direct Deposit Sign-Up Form (FMS Form 1200)

How to Complete the FMS Form 1200:

Payee must complete boxes A,B,C,D,E and F.

Please clearly print all information. Provide name(s) and address exactly as they appear on the Federal benefit recipient's benefit check.

Federal Benefit Recipient Information

Name of person entitled to government benefits (beneficiary).

If there is more than one person named on the check, such as a parent and a minor child, this will be the name of the minor child.

Representative Payee? Check appropriate box Yes or No.

If yes, enter Name of Representative Payee.

A representative payee is a person or institution that is legally entitled to receive payments on behalf of a beneficiary who has been deemed incapable of handing his/her own financial affairs. The majority of benefit recipients do not have representative payees. When a representative payee is present, both names will appear on the benefit check. Minor children receiving federal benefits should always have a representative payee. An example of a representative check payee is: Mary Smith for Jane R. Doe.

Provide name(s) and address exactly as they appear on the most recent check benefit.

Daytime Telephone Number of the person to contact if there are questions regarding the enrollment information provided on the form.

Social Security number of person entitled to government benefits (beneficiary).

If the benefits are for a minor child this will be the child's SSN. **This is never the representative payee's SSN.**

Bank or Credit Union Information

Depositor's Account Title - Name(s) as they appear on the bank account deposit will be made to.

The account title must include the name of the person authorized to receive the payment. (e.g. representative payee if applicable).

Indicate account type either Checking or Savings.

9-digit routing number. This is a 9-digit number used to denote which financial institution will receive the deposit. This number can be found in the bottom left hand corner of personal checks drawn upon that institute.

Account Number - this represents the account where the funds will be deposited. This may be up to 17 characters long. It may contain both numeric 0-9 and alphabetic characters A to Z.

Type of Payment (check only one box)

The appropriate box should be checked. Refer to the examples that follow to determine how to identify the appropriate payment type

Note: *You must use a separate form for each payment type or individual that is being enrolled.*

For payment types not listed on the Form 1200 please refer to the next section, Direct Deposit Sign-up Form (SF 1199A) for instruction on submitting enrollments for other payment types.

Claim Number or Check Number. One of these two items is required.

Claim number is an identifying number assigned by the paying agency to the benefit recipient. In many cases, this is the social security number the benefits are drawn upon followed by a series of letters or letters and numbers. For some agencies this may be a unique number that does not use the SSN. Claim numbers can typically be found on award letters issued by the paying agency, correspondence sent by the agency, or year end tax statements.

Check number is the 12-digit check number of the recipient's most recent benefit payment.

The check number is located in the upper right hand corner of the check. It is formatted as 4-digits a space and then 8-digits. (example: 2053 87654321)

Dollar amount of most recent benefit payment. This value is required. Indicate the dollar amount in dollars and cents of the most recent benefit payment which was received.

When Using Witnesses

When witnesses are used, they should sign to the right of the mark "X", and print the word "Witness" above their signature.

Power-of-Attorney

A person appointed as a power-of-attorney by the court cannot sign the FMS Form 1200 for the payee. The FMS Form 1200 is, in effect, a power-of-attorney and one power-of-attorney cannot execute a second power-of-attorney. The FMS Form 1200 can only be signed by the designated recipient or a representative payee. Questions regarding this item should be directed to the appropriate Federal Agency.

Agency / Payment Type	Recipient
Federal Housing Administration Debentures (Bureau of the Fiscal Service)	The Federal Housing Administration (FHA) issues these debentures in settlement of defaulted mortgages. The Federal Reserve Bank of Philadelphia maintains the system. Payments are made by Direct Deposit. For more information, recipients should contact Housing and Urban Development at (202) 708-3423, or write to: HUD 451 7th Street, SW Washington, DC 20410 Attn: multi-family or single family claims
Series H/HH Savings Bond Interest Payments (Bureau of the Fiscal Service)	Completes PD F 5396. Recipients should contact the Current Income Bond Branch, Bureau of the Fiscal Service, Parkersburg, WV 26102-2186 or visit _www.savingsbonds.gov_ to download the form.

*Note: Only send completed SF 1199A forms to the Federal Agency responsible for issuing the payment. The **Go Direct** Processing Center is unable to process the SF 1199A form and will be forced to reject them.*

Sample SF 1200, Front

Sign-Up Form for
Direct Deposit

You may also sign up online today at www.GoDirect.org
or call *Go Direct®* toll free at 1 (800) 333-1795

(for social security, railroad retirement board, civil (non-military)
retirement payments or VA **only**).

DIRECTIONS

Please read the information on page 2 before completing this form. **You must complete boxes A, B, C, D, E and F.**
Only complete this form to sign up for direct deposit if you are an individual, or a representative payee of an individual, who receives checks
for the following types of federal benefits: **social security, supplemental security income, railroad retirement, civil (non-military)
retirement, or VA (compensation or pension only). If you currently receive your payment by direct deposit you may not use
this form. Please refer to page 2 for further instructions.**

A. FEDERAL BENEFIT RECIPIENT INFORMATION
(print name[s] and address exactly as they appear on your benefit check)

NAME OF PERSON ENTITLED TO GOVERNMENT BENEFITS (BENEFICIARY)

REPRESENTATIVE PAYEE?
Yes [ ] *if yes, enter* No [ ]   NAME OF REPRESENTATIVE PAYEE
name at right

ADDRESS *(street, route, P.O. box, apartment number)*

CITY *(or APO/FPO)*   STATE   ZIP CODE

DAYTIME TELEPHONE NUMBER

(   )   -

SOCIAL SECURITY NUMBER OF PERSON ENTITLED TO GOVERNMENT BENEFITS
(BENEFICIARY)

SAMPLE CHECK *(bottom left corner)* ➡

B. BANK OR CREDIT UNION INFORMATION

DEPOSITOR ACCOUNT TITLE *(name[s] on account)*

ACCOUNT TYPE   ** 9-DIGIT ROUTING NUMBER
                    (see sample check below)
Checking [ ]   Savings [ ]

** ACCOUNT NUMBER *(see sample check below; do not include check number)*

** You may also attach a voided personal check. If you are depositing into a savings account, you
may need to contact your financial institution to obtain the routing and account numbers.

⑆111999087⑆ ⑈9876554321⑈ ⑉0001
ROUTING NUMBER   ACCOUNT NUMBER   CHECK NUMBER

C. TYPE OF PAYMENT *(check only one)* You must complete a separate form for each type of federal payment.

[ ] SOCIAL SECURITY   [ ] SUPPLEMENTAL SECURITY INCOME   [ ] VA (COMP/PENSION ONLY)

**For military, federal salary, veterans benefits or other federal payments
not available through *Go Direct*, please contact the paying agency
*(see page 2 for a partial list of paying agencies).***

RAILROAD RETIREMENT
(specify below)
Annuity [ ]   Unemployment [ ]
benefit   survivor benefit

CIVIL (NON-MILITARY) RETIREMENT
(specify below)
Retirement [ ]   Survivor [ ]
annuity   annuity

D. IDENTIFICATION

CLAIM NUMBER

OR

CHECK NUMBER (YOUR MOST RECENT PAYMENT)

⬅ In order to process your request, **either** the claim
number (found on documents from your paying
agency) **or** the check number from your last
payment (found in the upper right hand corner
of your Treasury check) **must be entered** at left.

E. PAYMENT VERIFICATION

*You must **also** enter the amount
of your last benefit payment.*

AMOUNT OF YOUR MOST RECENT PAYMENT

$ [   ] . [   ]

F. CERTIFICATION

I certify that I am entitled to receive the payment identified above, and that I have
read and understand the back of this form. In signing this form, I authorize this
payment to be sent to the financial institution named in Part B above, to be
deposited into the account above.

SIGNATURE   DATE

FOR JOINT ACCOUNT HOLDERS

I certify that I have read the SPECIAL NOTICE TO JOINT ACCOUNT
HOLDERS on the back of this form.

SIGNATURE   DATE

**Be sure to complete all sections of this form.
Otherwise, the form cannot be processed.
Return the completed form to:**

Go Direct Processing Center

This form is **only** to be used for switching from check payments to direct deposit of certain federal
benefits listed in Box C. Use of this form for any other purposes will result in the form being rejected.

Contact your paying agency to:
• Update your name or address

Sample SF 1200, Back

PLEASE READ THIS CAREFULLY

PRIVACY ACT NOTICE
Your social security number and the other information requested will allow the federal government to make payments to you by direct deposit. This collection of information is authorized by Title 31 of the United States Code, Section 3332(g). Also, Executive Order 9397, November 22, 1943, authorizes the use of your social security number. Your social security number is requested to ensure the accurate identification and retention of records pertaining to you and to distinguish you from other recipients of federal payments.

This information will be disclosed to the Department of the Treasury or another disbursing official to process federal payments to you by direct deposit. This information may also be disclosed to a court, congressional committee or another government agency as authorized or required by federal law and to your financial institution to verify receipt of your federal payments. Although providing the requested information is voluntary, your direct deposit payment may be delayed or Treasury may be unable to send it if you fail to provide the information.

SPECIAL NOTICE TO JOINT ACCOUNT HOLDERS
If your account is a joint account and receives direct deposit benefit payments, you must inform the federal agency and the financial institution of the death of a beneficiary. Payments sent by direct deposit after the date of death or ineligibility of a beneficiary (except for salary payments) must be returned to the federal agency. The federal agency will then determine if the survivor is eligible for benefits.

CANCELLATION
Your payment will be sent by direct deposit until the federal agency that issues the payments is notified to cancel, such as in the case of death or legal incapacity of the person receiving the payment.

Your financial institution may cancel your direct deposit authorization. Your financial institution is required to give you written notice 30 days in advance of the cancellation date. If this occurs, you must notify the federal agency that the direct deposit authorization was cancelled.

Please contact your paying agency to:
- Update your name or address
- Change your account information if you already receive your payment by direct deposit, or
- Sign up for direct deposit for military, federal salary, veterans benefits, or other federal payments not processed by *Go Direct*

Department of Veterans Affairs	**Railroad Retirement Board**
(877) 838-2778	(Automated System)
(800) 827-1000	(800) 808-0772
(800) 829-4833 TDD	(312) 751-4701 TTY
Social Security Administration	**Office of Personnel Management**
(800) 772-1213	(888) 767-6738
(800) 325-0778 TTY	(800) 878-5707 TDD

BURDEN ESTIMATE STATEMENT

The estimated average time (burden hours) associated with filling out this paperwork is 10 minutes per respondent or recordkeeper, depending on individual circumstances. Comments concerning the accuracy of this time estimate and suggestions for reducing the burden should be directed to the Financial Management Service, Administrative Programs Division, Records and Information Management Program, 3700 East-West Highway, Room 135, Hyattsville, MD 20782. THIS ADDRESS SHOULD ONLY BE USED FOR COMMENTS AND/OR SUGGESTIONS CONCERNING THE AMOUNT OF TIME SPENT COLLECTING THE DATA. DO NOT SEND THE COMPLETED PAPERWORK TO THE ADDRESS ABOVE FOR PROCESSING.

(2)

Social Security Administration

Example 1:
Single Payee

United States Treasury 15-51/000

Month	Day	Year
03	01	07

PHILADELPHIA, PA

Check No.
5000 41571922

Pay to
the order of JOHN DOE
123 MAPLE DRIVE
WOODSTOCK VA 23456

SOC SEC
FOR FEB

DOLLARS	CTS
$****371	84

VOID AFTER ONE YEAR

NOT NEGOTIABLE

Sign-Up Form for
Direct Deposit

You may also sign up online today at www.GoDirect.org
or call *Go Direct®* toll free at 1 (800) 333 1795

(for social security, railroad retirement board, civil (non-military)
retirement payments or VA **only**).

DIRECTIONS

Please read the information on page 2 before completing this form. **You must complete boxes A, B, C, D, E and F.**
Only complete this form to sign up for direct deposit if you are an individual, or a representative payee of an individual, who receives checks
for the following types of federal benefits: **social security, supplemental security income, railroad retirement, civil (non-military)
retirement, or VA (compensation or pension only). If you currently receive your payment by direct deposit you may not use
this form. Please refer to page 2 for further instructions.**

A. FEDERAL BENEFIT RECIPIENT INFORMATION
(print name[s] and address exactly as they appear on your benefit check)

NAME OF PERSON ENTITLED TO GOVERNMENT BENEFITS (BENEFICIARY)

REPRESENTATIVE PAYEE? Yes [ ] *(if yes, enter name at right)* No [ ]   NAME OF REPRESENTATIVE PAYEE

ADDRESS *(street, route, PO box, apartment number)*

CITY *(or APO/FPO)*   STATE   ZIP CODE

DAYTIME TELEPHONE NUMBER
(   )

SOCIAL SECURITY NUMBER OF PERSON ENTITLED TO GOVERNMENT BENEFITS
(BENEFICIARY)
[   ] - [ ] - [   ]

SAMPLE CHECK *(bottom left corner)* ➡

B. BANK OR CREDIT UNION INFORMATION

DEPOSITOR ACCOUNT TITLE *(name[s] on account)*

ACCOUNT TYPE   Checking [ ]   Savings [ ]   ** 9 DIGIT ROUTING NUMBER
(see sample check below)

** ACCOUNT NUMBER *(see sample check below; do not include check number)*

** You may also attach a voided personal check If you are depositing into a savings account, you
may need to contact your financial institution to obtain the routing and account numbers

⑈ 111999087 ⑈ ⑆ 9876554321 ⑈ ⑆ 0001
ROUTING NUMBER   ACCOUNT NUMBER   CHECK NUMBER

C. TYPE OF PAYMENT *(check only one)*   You must complete a separate form for each type of federal payment.

[ ] SOCIAL SECURITY   [ ] SUPPLEMENTAL SECURITY INCOME   [ ] VA (COMP/PENSION ONLY)

For military, federal salary, veterans benefits or other federal payments
not available through Go Direct, please contact the paying agency
(see page 2 for a partial list of paying agencies).

RAILROAD RETIREMENT *(specify below)*
Annuity benefit [ ]   Unemployment survivor benefit [ ]

CIVIL (NON MILITARY) RETIREMENT *(specify below)*
Retirement annuity [ ]   Survivor annuity [ ]

D. IDENTIFICATION

CLAIM NUMBER
[   ]   **OR**

CHECK NUMBER (YOUR MOST RECENT PAYMENT) ⬅
[   ]

In order to process your request, *either* the claim
number (found on documents from your paying
agency) *or* the check number from your last
payment (found in the upper right-hand corner
of your Treasury check) **must be entered** at left.

E. PAYMENT VERIFICATION

You must **also** enter the amount
of your last benefit payment.

AMOUNT OF YOUR MOST RECENT PAYMENT
$ [   ] . [   ]

F. CERTIFICATION

I certify that I am entitled to receive the payment identified above, and that I have
read and understand the back of this form. In signing this form, I authorize this
payment to be sent to the financial institution named in Part B above, to be
deposited into the account above.

SIGNATURE   DATE

FOR JOINT ACCOUNT HOLDERS

I certify that I have read the SPECIAL NOTICE TO JOINT ACCOUNT
HOLDERS on the back of this form.

SIGNATURE   DATE

**Be sure to complete all sections of this form.
Otherwise, the form cannot be processed.
Return the completed form to:**

Go Direct Processing Center
U.S. Department of the Treasury
P.O Box 650527
Dallas, TX 75265-0527

This form is **only** to be used for switching from check payments to direct deposit of certain federal
benefits listed in Box C. Use of this form for any other purposes will result in the form being rejected.

Contact your paying agency to:
- Update your name or address
- Change your account information if you already receive your payment by direct deposit, or
- Sign up for direct deposit for military, federal salary, veterans benefits, or other federal
  payments not processed by *Go Direct*

Social Security Administration

Example 2: Representative Payee

SF 1200 Examples

United States Treasury 15-51/000

Month	Day	Year
03	02	07

PHILADELPHIA, PA

Check No.
5000 41571922

Pay to the order of

JANE DOE FOR
JOHN DOE
123 MAPLE DRIVE
WOODSTOCK VA 23456

SOC SEC FOR FEB

DOLLARS	CTS
$****371	84

VOID AFTER ONE YEAR

NOT NEGOTIABLE

Sign-Up Form for
Direct Deposit
of Federal Benefit Payments

You may also sign up online today at www.GoDirect.org or call *Go Direct®* toll free at 1 (800) 333 1795

(for social security, railroad retirement board, civil (non-military) retirement payments or VA **only**).

FMS Form 1200 *(January 2008)*　　　OMB No. 1510-0007

DIRECTIONS

Please read the information on page 2 before completing this form. **You must complete boxes A, B, C, D, E and F.**

Only complete this form to sign up for direct deposit if you are an individual, or a representative payee of an individual, who receives checks for the following types of federal benefits: **social security, supplemental security income, railroad retirement, civil (non-military) retirement, or VA (compensation or pension only)**. If you currently receive your payment by direct deposit you may not use this form. Please refer to page 2 for further instructions.

A. FEDERAL BENEFIT RECIPIENT INFORMATION
(print name[s] and address exactly as they appear on your benefit check)

NAME OF PERSON ENTITLED TO GOVERNMENT BENEFITS (BENEFICIARY)

REPRESENTATIVE PAYEE? Yes [if yes an er name at right] No　　NAME OF REPRESENTATIVE PAYEE

ADDRESS *(street, route, PO box, apartment number)*

CITY *(or APO/FPO)*　　STATE　　ZIP CODE

DAYTIME TELEPHONE NUMBER

( )　　—

SOCIAL SECURITY NUMBER OF PERSON ENTITLED TO GOVERNMENT BENEFITS (BENEFICIARY)

—　　—

B. BANK OR CREDIT UNION INFORMATION

DEPOSITOR ACCOUNT TITLE *(name[s] on account)*

ACCOUNT TYPE　　** 9 DIGIT ROUTING NUMBER *(see sample check below)*

Checking　　Savings

** ACCOUNT NUMBER *(see sample check below; do not include check number)*

** You may also attach a voded personal check. If you are depositing into a savings account, you may need to contact your financial institution to obtain the routing and account numbers

SAMPLE CHECK *(bottom left corner)* ➡

|:111999087|: 9876554321 |"|0001|
ROUTING NUMBER　　ACCOUNT NUMBER　　CHECK NUMBER

C. TYPE OF PAYMENT *(check only one)*　You must complete a separate form for each type of federal payment.

SOCIAL SECURITY　　SUPPLEMENTAL SECURITY INCOME　　VA (COMP/PENSION ONLY)

RAILROAD RETIREMENT *(specify below)*
Annuity benefit　　Unemployment survivor benefit

CIVIL (NON MILITARY) RETIREMENT *(specify below)*
Retirement annuity　　Survivor annuity

or military, federal salary, veterans benefits or other federal payments not available through *Go Direct*, please contact the paying agency *(see page 2 for a partial list of paying agencies)*.

D. IDENTIFICATION

CLAIM NUMBER

OR

CHECK NUMBER (YOUR MOST RECENT PAYMENT)

In order to process your request, **either the claim number** *(found on documents from your paying agency)* **or the check number from your last payment** *(found in the upper right-hand corner of your Treasury check)* **must be entered** at left.

E. PAYMENT VERIFICATION

*You must **also** enter the amount of your last benefit payment.*

AMOUNT OF YOUR MOST RECENT PAYMENT

$

F. CERTIFICATION

I certify that I am entitled to receive the payment identified above, and that I have read and understand the back of this form. In signing this form, I authorize this payment to be sent to the financial institution named in Part B above, to be deposited into the account above.

SIGNATURE　　DATE

FOR JOINT ACCOUNT HOLDERS

I certify that I have read the SPECIAL NOTICE TO JOINT ACCOUNT HOLDERS on the back of this form.

SIGNATURE　　DATE

Be sure to complete all sections of this form. Otherwise, the form cannot be processed. Return the completed form to:

**Go Direct Processing Center
U.S. Department of the Treasury
P.O Box 650527
Dallas, TX 75265-0527**

This form is **only** to be used for switching from check payments to direct deposit of certain federal benefits listed in Box C. Use of this form for any other purposes will result in the form being rejected.

Contact your paying agency to:
- Update your name or address
- Change your account information if you already receive your payment by direct deposit, or
- Sign up for direct deposit for military, federal salary, veterans benefits, or other federal payments not processed by *Go Direct*

D. Direct Deposit Sign-Up Form (SF 1199A)

How to Complete the SF 1199A:

Section 1- To be completed by the payee

The financial institution should verify that all information on this portion of the form is correct.

The financial institution needs to be aware of the following special items:

Name of the Person(s) Entitled to Payment (Box B)

In most cases, this will be the name of the payee. Refer to the appropriate Federal agency examples to determine what information to enter for recurring benefit payments.

Claim or Payroll ID Number (Box C)

Payment claim numbers are generally not printed on a recipient's check. Claim numbers may be found on other documents provided by the recipient's paying agency(s) such as: award letters, yearly tax statements or other general correspondence.

Claim Number Prefix

A prefix is one or more letters preceding the claim number. These characters indicate the type of claim for which benefits are being paid. For an explanation of the meaning of a prefix, contact the Federal agency authorizing the payment.

Claim Number

A number that identifies the recipient's records at the Federal agency that authorizes the payment: usually a Social Security number or an equivalent identification number.

Claim Number Suffix

A suffix is one or more characters (letters or numbers) following a claim number. These characters indicate the payment type or the payee's relationship to the individual who the benefits are being drawn. For a full explanation of a suffix, contact the Federal agency authorizing the payment.

> **Example:**
> **VA Compensation, Pension and Education . .123-45-6789 00**

Note: The claim number suffix for VA Compensation, Pension and Education benefit payments reflects the entitlement status of the beneficiary. For example, suffix '00' means the veteran, and '10' means the spouse of the veteran.

Claim/Payroll ID Table

The table below shoes what to enter on the SF 1199A for the Claim or Payroll ID Number (BOX C) for the various payment types.

Payment Type	Prefix	Claim Number	Suffix
Allotments (Savings and Discretionary	Leave Blank	Social Security Number or Payroll ID Number	Leave Blank
Black Lung (Department of Labor)	Leave Blank	Social Security Number	2 characters following the Social Security Number
Central Intelligence Agency / Annuity	Leave Blank	Social Security Number	Leave Blank
Federal Employee Workers' Compensation (Department of Labor)	Leave Blank	Case number assigned by the Federal agency	Leave Blank
Federal Salary / Military Civilian Pay	Leave Blank	Social Security Number or Payroll ID Number	Leave Blank
Longshore and Harbor Workers' Compensation (Department of Labor)	Leave Blank	File number assigned by the Federal agency	Leave Blank
Military Active Duty and Allotments	Leave Blank	Social Security Number	Leave Blank
Military Retirement and Annuity	Leave Blank	Social Security Number	Leave Blank
Miner's Benefit (Department of Labor)	Leave Blank	Social Security Number	Leave Blank
Savings Bond Agency's Fee (Bureau of the Fiscal Service)	Leave Blank	Issuing or paying agency code assigned to the financial institution	1- or 2-digit number following the Social Security Number
Series H/HH Savings Bond Interest Payments (Bureau of the Fiscal Service)	Leave Blank	Social Security Number	Leave Blank

Claim/Payroll ID Table (continued)

The table below shoes what to enter on the SF 1199A for the Claim or Payroll ID Number (BOX C) for the various payment types.

Payment Type	Prefix	Claim Number	Suffix
Veterans Compensation, Pension or Education	Leave Blank	8-digit or 9-digit Social Security Number	Always a 2-digit number
Veterans Life Insurance	1 to 2 letters	4- to 8-digit number	None or a 2-digit number

Depositor Account Number (Box E)

• If account numbers are not used, then insert name or other identification in the box.

• Use only letters of the alphabet, digits 0-9

• Use up to 17 characters

Type of Payment (Box F)

The appropriate box should be checked

If the .payment type is not included in the list, then check "Other" and enter the payment type in the blank.

For military payments, enter the name of the military branch in the blank next to the payment type checked.

Payee / Joint Payee Certification (Box F)

IF...	THEN...
there is only one payee, who could be a representative payee*	only his/her signature is required
joint payees complete the form	both must sign the form
the payee's signature is made be a mark "X"	it must be witnessed by two persons who sign and date the form.

See Glossary, Chapter 9

Joint Account Holders' Certification (Optional)

Federal agencies do not require signatures in this block; however, some financial institutions do.

If the signature is made by a mark "X", it must be witnessed by two persons who sign and date the form.

When Using Witnesses

When witnesses are used, they should sign to the right of the mark "X", and print the word "Witness" above their signature.

Power-of-Attorney

A person appointed as a power-of-attorney by the court cannot sign the SF 1199A for the payee. The SF 1199A is, in effect, a power-of-attorney and one power-of-attorney cannot execute a second power-of-attorney. The SF 1199A can only be signed by the designated recipient or a representative payee. Questions regarding this item should be directed to the appropriate Federal agency.

Section 2 · To Be Completed by the Payee or the Financial Institution

The financial institution should verify that the name and address of the Federal agency that authorized the payment is used.

For a listing of addresses, refer to Chapter 8, *Contracts*.

Note: *Do not send enrollment forms to the FInancial Management Service (FMS). The FMS does not process enrollment forms except for its own employees.*

Section 3 · To Be Completed by the Financial Institution

ENTER the...

- financial institution's name and address
- financial institution's Routing Number
- depositor's account title
  (this title must include the name of the person authorized to receive the payment)
- financial institution representative's name, signature, telephone number, and current date.

What Actions Should Take Place Before Filing the SF 1199A?

This checklist can be used to verify that all information entered on the enrollment form is complete and accurate.

Verify	CHECK ✓
Name of person(s) entitled to payment*	
Claim or payroll ID number. Refer to CLAIM OR PAYROLL ID NUMBER*	
Type of depositor account	
Depositor account number	
Type of payment	
Proper signatures	

Note: *Make sure the Federal agency that authorizes the payment is entered, not the Financial Management Service. The FInancial Management Service does not process enrollment forms, except for its own employees.*

Verify   CHECK ✓

Federal agency name and address*
Name and address of financial institution
Routing Number and check digit

Depositor account title*
Make sure it includes the name of the person authorized to receive the payment

Note: *Items marked with an asterisk (*) are where most errors occur.*

Important Information for New Direct Deposit Recipients

1. The financial institution should inform the recipient that he/she will continue to receive checks or deposits at his/her current payment address of record until the Direct Deposit enrollment is processed.

2. The financial institution should inform the recipient on how to verify receipt of a Direct Deposit payment.

3. The financial institution should inform the recipient to notify the Federal agency of any address changes after Direct Deposit begins, since important information about the payment will be sent to the individual's home address. Some Federal agencies are required to stop payments if mail to the home address is returned and the recipient or beneficiary cannot be located.

4. The financial institution should inform the recipient that it is important to notify both the Federal agency and the financial institution if the recipient or beneficiary dies or becomes legally incapacitated.

5. The financial institution should inform the recipient that if he/she is changing financial institutions, his/her old account should not be closed until Direct Deposit begins into the new account. Make sure the recipient understands that changing financial institutions requires filling out a new Direct Deposit enrollment.

How Are Forms Distributed?

Government Agency Copy Delivered by the employee to his/her payroll office, or mailed to the Federal agency that authorizes the payment.	DO NOT SEND THE FORM TO THE FINANCIAL MANAGEMENT SERVICE (See Appendix 2 at the end of this chapter for agency addresses and phone numbers.)
Financial Institution Copy Held by the financial institution	There is no official retention period for the SF 1199A. It is recommended that financial institutions retain this form at least until receipt of the first payment.
Payee(s) Copy Held by the recipient.	

What to do if Direct Deposit does not begin

Follow these steps if Direct Deposit does not begin within the specified time period.

Step	Action
1	Ask recipient if the enrollment authorization has been revoked. If yes, no further action is required. If no, and Direct Deposit is still desired, go to Step 2.
2	Make a copy of the completed enrollment form from the financial institution's file copy. *Note: Verify that all the information on the form is correct.*
3	Send a copy of the form and a letter stating that the recipient still wants to receive Direct Deposit to the Federal agency that authorizes the payment.
4	Remind recipient(s) that checks will continue to be sent to his/her home address of record until Direct Deposit begins.

Sample SF 1199A, front

Standard Form 1199A
(Rev. June 1987)
Prescribed by Treasury
Department
Treasury Dept. Cir. 1076

OMB No. 1510–0007

DIRECT DEPOSIT SIGN-UP FORM

DIRECTIONS

- To sign up for Direct Deposit, the payee is to read the back of this form and fill in the information requested in Sections 1 and 2. Then take or mail this form to the financial institution. The financial institution will verify the information in Sections 1 and 2, and will complete Section 3. The completed form will be returned to the Government agency identified below.

- A separate form must be completed for each type of payment to be sent by Direct Deposit.

- The claim number and type of payment are printed on Government checks. (See the sample check on the back of this form.) This information is also stated on beneficiary/annuitant award letters and other documents from the Government agency.

- Payees must keep the Government agency informed of any address changes in order to receive important information about benefits and to remain qualified for payments.

SECTION 1 *(TO BE COMPLETED BY PAYEE)*

A NAME OF PAYEE *(last, first, middle initial)*

ADDRESS *(street, route, P.O. Box, APO/FPO)*

CITY   STATE   ZIP CODE

TELEPHONE NUMBER
AREA CODE

B NAME OF PERSON(S) ENTITLED TO PAYMENT

C CLAIM OR PAYROLL ID NUMBER

Prefix   Suffix

D TYPE OF DEPOSITOR ACCOUNT ☐ CHECKING ☐ SAVINGS

E DEPOSITOR ACCOUNT NUMBER

F TYPE OF PAYMENT *(Check only one)*
☐ Social Security
☐ Supplemental Security Income
☐ Railroad Retirement
☐ Civil Service Retirement (OPM)
☐ VA Compensation or Pension
☐ Fed Salary/Mil. Civilian Pay
☐ Mil. Active _____
☐ Mil. Retire. _____
☐ Mil. Survivor _____
☐ Other _____
(specify)

G THIS BOX FOR ALLOTMENT OF PAYMENT ONLY *(if applicable)*

TYPE	AMOUNT

PAYEE/JOINT PAYEE CERTIFICATION

I certify that I am entitled to the payment identified above, and that I have read and understood the back of this form. In signing this form, I authorize my payment to be sent to the financial institution named below to be deposited to the designated account.

JOINT ACCOUNT HOLDERS' CERTIFICATION *(optional)*

I certify that I have read and understood the back of this form, including the SPECIAL NOTICE TO JOINT ACCOUNT HOLDERS.

SIGNATURE	DATE	SIGNATURE	DATE
SIGNATURE	DATE	SIGNATURE	DATE

SECTION 2 *(TO BE COMPLETED BY PAYEE OR FINANCIAL INSTITUTION)*

GOVERNMENT AGENCY NAME   GOVERNMENT AGENCY ADDRESS

SECTION 3 *(TO BE COMPLETED BY FINANCIAL INSTITUTION)*

NAME AND ADDRESS OF FINANCIAL INSTITUTION

ROUTING NUMBER   CHECK DIGIT

DEPOSITOR ACCOUNT TITLE

FINANCIAL INSTITUTION CERTIFICATION

I confirm the identity of the above-named payee(s) and the account number and title. As representative of the above-named financial institution, I certify that the financial institution agrees to receive and deposit the payment identified above in accordance with 31 CFR Parts 240, 209, and 210.

PRINT OR TYPE REPRESENTATIVE'S NAME	SIGNATURE OF REPRESENTATIVE	TELEPHONE NUMBER	DATE

Financial institutions should refer to the GREEN BOOK for further instructions.

THE FINANCIAL INSTITUTION SHOULD MAIL THE COMPLETED FORM TO THE GOVERNMENT AGENCY IDENTIFIED ABOVE.

NSN 7540-01-058-0224

1199–204

GOVERNMENT AGENCY COPY

Social Security Administration

SF 1199A Examples

Example 1: Single Payee

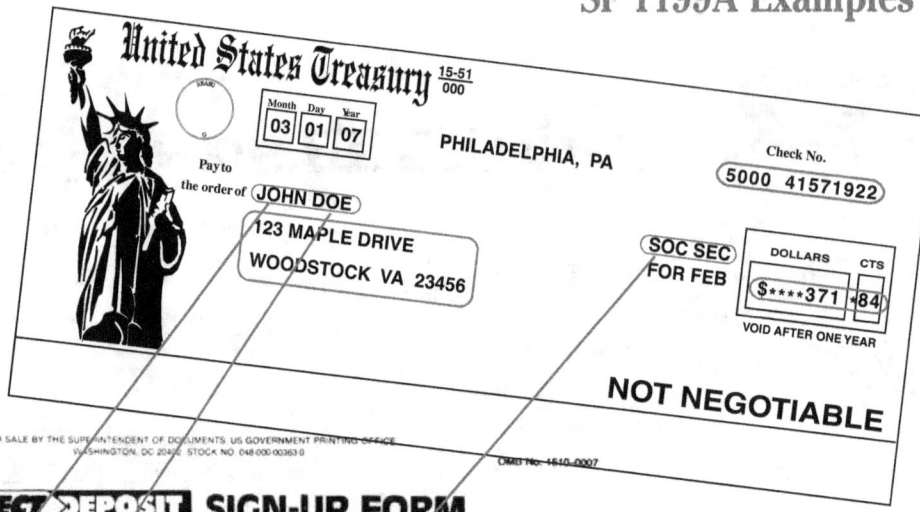

Standard Form 1199A
(Rev. June 1987)
Prescribed by Treasury Department
Treasury Dept. Cir. 1076

DIRECT DEPOSIT SIGN-UP FORM

DIRECTIONS

- To sign up for Direct Deposit, the payee is to read the back of this form and fill in the information requested in Sections 1 and 2. Then take or mail this form to the financial institution. The financial institution will verify the information in Sections 1 and 2, and will complete Section 3. The completed form will be returned to the Government agency identified below.

- A separate form must be completed for each type of payment to be sent by Direct Deposit.

- The claim number and type of payment are printed on Government checks. (See the sample check on the back of this form.) This information is also stated on beneficiary/annuitant award letters and other documents from the Government agency.

- Payees must keep the Government agency informed of any address changes in order to receive important information about benefits and to remain qualified for payments.

SECTION 1 (TO BE COMPLETED BY PAYEE)

A NAME OF PAYEE (last, first, middle initial)
Doe, John

ADDRESS (street, route, P.O. Box, APO/FPO)
123 Maple Drive

CITY   STATE   ZIP CODE
Woodstock   VA   23456

TELEPHONE NUMBER
AREA CODE (703) 555-1234

B NAME OF PERSON(S) ENTITLED TO PAYMENT
John Doe

C CLAIM OR PAYROLL ID NUMBER
123-45-6789   A
Prefix   Suffix

D TYPE OF DEPOSITOR ACCOUNT   ☐ CHECKING   ☐ SAVINGS

E DEPOSITOR ACCOUNT NUMBER
1 2 3 4 5

F TYPE OF PAYMENT (Check only one)
☒ Social Security
☐ Supplemental Security Income
☐ Railroad Retirement
☐ Civil Service Retirement (OPM)
☐ VA Compensation or Pension
☐ Fed Salary/Mil. Civilian Pay
☐ Mil. Active _____
☐ Mil. Retire _____
☐ Mil. Survivor _____
☐ Other _____
(specify)

G THIS BOX FOR ALLOTMENT OF PAYMENT ONLY (if applicable)
TYPE   AMOUNT

PAYEE/JOINT PAYEE CERTIFICATION
I certify that I am entitled to the payment identified above, and that I have read and understood the back of this form. In signing this form, I authorize my payment to be sent to the financial institution named below to be deposited to the designated account.

SIGNATURE *John Doe*   DATE 3-1-00
SIGNATURE   DATE

JOINT ACCOUNT HOLDERS' CERTIFICATION (optional)
I certify that I have read and understood the back of this form, including the SPECIAL NOTICE TO JOINT ACCOUNT HOLDERS.

SIGNATURE   DATE
SIGNATURE   DATE

SECTION 2 (TO BE COMPLETED BY PAYEE OR FINANCIAL INSTITUTION)

GOVERNMENT AGENCY NAME
Social Security Administration

GOVERNMENT AGENCY ADDRESS
Enter the address of the local SSA District Office.

SECTION 3 (TO BE COMPLETED BY FINANCIAL INSTITUTION)

NAME AND ADDRESS OF FINANCIAL INSTITUTION
Friendly Financial Institution
100 Main Street
Woodstock, VA 23456

ROUTING NUMBER
1 2 3 4 5 6 7 8   CHECK DIGIT 9

DEPOSITOR ACCOUNT TITLE
John Doe

FINANCIAL INSTITUTION CERTIFICATION
I confirm the identity of the above-named payee(s) and the account number and title. As representative of the above-named financial institution, I certify that the financial institution agrees to receive and deposit the payment identified above in accordance with 31 CFR Parts 240, 209, and 210.

PRINT OR TYPE REPRESENTATIVE'S NAME
A.B. Smith

SIGNATURE OF REPRESENTATIVE
A.B. Smith

TELEPHONE NUMBER
(703) 555-1000

DATE
3-1-00

Financial institutions should refer to the GREEN BOOK for further instructions.
THE FINANCIAL INSTITUTION SHOULD MAIL THE COMPLETED FORM TO THE GOVERNMENT AGENCY IDENTIFIED ABOVE.

NSN 7540-01-058-0224

1199-204

GOVERNMENT AGENCY COPY

Note: *This example applies to Social Security and Supplemental Social Security Income payments.*

E. Federal Financial EDI (FEDI) Payments / Vendor Payments

Overview

EDI is defined as the computer to computer transmission of routine business information in a standard format. Federal payments made using Financial EDI or FEDI refers to the electronic transfer of funds and payment-related information. The Federal government uses FEDI for payments it makes to businesses, which provide goods and services to Federal agencies, and other payment recipients, such as State/local governments and educational institutions. For more information, see *http://fms.treas.gov/pdf/ffedidui.pdf*.

Provisions of the Debt Collection Improvement Act of 1996 require that the majority of Federal payments be made by EFT. These payments include corporate payments to companies providing goods or services to the Federal government. This requirement impacts every Federal government vendor regardless of the size of the company or the goods or services provided.

The Federal government currently uses the two NACHA corporate payment formats for vendor payments. These formats are:

• **CCD+** for single invoice payments. Contains one 80-character addenda record for transmitting the invoice information.

• **CTX** for single or multiple payments. Allows for 9,999 addends records for the consolidation of multiple invoices in one payment.

Delivery of Remittance (Addenda) Information

The NACHA Operating Rules address the delivery of remittance information contained in the addenda record. At the recipient's request, financial institutions must provide the remittance information by the opening of business on the second banking day following the settlement date of the entry. This impacts all financial institutions processing ACH payments. The remittance information may be provided via a paper report, fax, e-mail, electronic transmission, or any other means negotiated between the recipient and the financial institution.

To perform this key role, it is imperative that the financial institution work closely with its corporate customers who may have business relationships with the Federal government. The following issues should be discussed with your corporate customers:

• How to deliver the remittance information to the customer

• When to deliver the remittance information to the customer

• What specific information to provide to the customer

• What fees, if any, are associated with this service

Enrollment

The ACH Vendor/Miscellaneous Payment Enrollment Form (SF 3881) is an optional three-part form that Federal agencies may use to enroll their vendors in the FEDI program (similar agency-specific forms or abbreviated check insert forms are also used). Federal agencies will stock the form and provide the form to vendors to initiate the enrollment process. Federal agencies will also discuss with the vendor the ACH payment format (CCD+ or CTX) to be used to transmit the payment. Also, the Federal agency and the vendor will determine the remittance information (e.g., the invoice number, discount terms) to be included in the addenda record.

The ACH Vendor/Miscellaneous Payment Enrollment Form (SF 2881) is available at *http://www.fms.treas.gov/pdf/3881.pdf*.

Enrollment Checklist

The table below is a checklist to assist the financial institution in enrolling a vendor in the FEDI program.

Action	CHECK ✓
Verify that the ACH format selected in the Agency Information section on the SF 3881 can be accepted and processed by the financial institution	
Agree on HOW and WHEN remittance information (e.g., invoice number) provided by the Federal agency in the addenda record will be passed to the vendor once it is received by the financial institution	

 Note: The agreement is reached by analyzing recipient requirements and comparing those requirements against the level of support the institution can provide.

Provide an example of how the addenda information will appear; or,	
Explain what type(s) of information to look for when the addenda information is received.	

 Note: The vendor must be able to understand the information to properly identify the payment.

Complete the Financial Institution Information section of the SF 3881.	

How to Complete the SF 3881

Agency Information

The Agency Information section of the form is completed by the Federal agency.

Payee/Company Information

The Payee/Company Information of the form is completed by the vendor or the financial institution, as appropriate.

Financial Institution Information

We suggest that the Financial Institution Information section of the form be completed by the financial institution as follows:

• the name and address of the financial institution

• the name and telephone number of the ACH contact

• the Routing Number used to receive ACH payments

• the depositor account title

• the depositor account number, lockbox number (if applicable)

• an "X" in the appropriate type of account box

• the signature, title, and telephone number of the financial institution representative

Form Distribution

The vendor will return the original SF 3881 to the Federal agency. The financial institution and the vendor each keep one copy of the form.

Pointers for Completing the SF 3881 Form

To answer the questions that vendors and agencies have raised when completing the vendor enrollment form and prevent some of the mistakes that have occurred, the FMS presents these additional pointers:

• The Federal Agency initiates the SF 3881 form to enroll its vendors to receive payment by electronic funds transfer.

• A vendor must complete a separate enrollment form (SF 3881) for each agency with which it does business.

• In the Agency Information Section, the term "AGENCY IDENTIFIER" means the acronym by which the agency is known. For example, the "AGENCY IDENTIFIER" for the Financial Management Service is FMS.

• In the Payee/Company Information Section, it should be noted that the "TAXPAYER ID NO." may be used by the government to collect and report on any delinquent amounts arising out of the offerer's relationship with the government (31 U.S.C. 2201 (c) (3)).

• The financial institution and the vendor should each keep a copy of the completed form.

• The vendor should return the completed SF 3881 to the agency that initiated the form.

Sample SF 3881, Front

<table>
<tr><td colspan="2" align="center">**ACH VENDOR/MISCELLANEOUS PAYMENT
ENROLLMENT FORM**</td><td>OMB No. 1510-0056
Expiration Date 01/31/2000</td></tr>
</table>

This form is used for Automated Clearing House (ACH) payments with an addendum record that contains payment-related information processed through the Vendor Express Program. Recipients of these payments should bring this information to the attention of their financial institution when presenting this form for completion.

PRIVACY ACT STATEMENT

The following information is provided to comply with the Privacy Act of 1974 (P.L. 93-579). All information collected on this form is required under the provisions of 31 U.S.C. 3322 and 31 CFR 210. This information will be used by the Treasury Department to transmit payment data, by electronic means to vendor's financial institution. Failure to provide the requested information may delay or prevent the receipt of payments through the Automated Clearing House Payment System.

AGENCY INFORMATION

FEDERAL PROGRAM AGENCY

AGENCY IDENTIFIER: AGENCY LOCATION CODE (ALC):   ACH FORMAT:
☐ CCD +   ☐ CTX

ADDRESS:

CONTACT PERSON NAME: TELEPHONE NUMBER:
( )

ADDITIONAL INFORMATION:

PAYEE/COMPANY INFORMATION

NAME   SSN NO. OR TAXPAYER ID NO.

ADDRESS

CONTACT PERSON NAME: TELEPHONE NUMBER:
( )

FINANCIAL INSTITUTION INFORMATION

NAME:

ADDRESS:

ACH COORDINATOR NAME: TELEPHONE NUMBER:
( )

NINE-DIGIT ROUTING TRANSIT NUMBER: — — — — —

DEPOSITOR ACCOUNT TITLE:

DEPOSITOR ACCOUNT NUMBER: LOCKBOX NUMBER:

TYPE OF ACCOUNT:
☐ CHECKING   ☐ SAVINGS   ☐ LOCKBOX

SIGNATURE AND TITLE OF AUTHORIZED OFFICIAL: TELEPHONE NUMBER:
(Could be the same as ACH Coordinator)
( )

NSN 7540-01-274-9925   3881-103   **FINANCIAL INSTITUTION COPY**   SF 3881 (Rev 12/90)
Prescribed by Department of Treasury
31 U S C 3322; 31 CFR 210

Sample SF 3881, Back

Instructions for Completing SF 3881 Form

1. Agency Information Section - Federal agency prints or types the name and address of the Federal program agency originating the vendor/miscellaneous payment, agency identifier, agency location code, contact person name and telephone number of the agency. Also, the appropriate box for ACH format is checked.

2. Payee/Company Information Section - Payee prints or types the name of the payee/company and address that will receive ACH vendor/miscellaneous payments, social security or taxpayer ID number, and contact person name and telephone number of the payee/company. Payee also verifies depositor account number, account title, and type of account entered by your financial institution in the Financial Institution Information Section.

3. Financial Institution Information Section - Financial institution prints or types the name and address of the payee/company's financial institution who will receive the ACH payment, ACH coordinator name and telephone number, nine-digit routing transit number, depositor (payee/company) account title and account number. Also, the box for type of account is checked, and the signature, title, and telephone number of the appropriate financial institution official are included.

Burden Estimate Statement

The estimated average burden associated with this collection of information is 15 minutes per respondent or recordkeeper, depending on individual circumstances. Comments concerning the accuracy of this burden estimate and suggestions for reducing this burden should be directed to the Financial Management Service, Facilities Management Division, Property and Supply Branch, Room B-101, 3700 East West Highway, Hyattsville, MD 20782 and the Office of Management and Budget, Paperwork Reduction Project (1510-0056), Washington, DC 20503.

F. Enrollment Desktop Guide

The appendix to the Green Book should be helpful to Financial Institutions who are trying to understand the differences between the traditional NACHA rules and the rules specifically for government payments. Use this desktop guide in conjunction with using the ACH entry class code ENR to enroll recipients of Federal benefit payments for Direct Deposit. It can be used to for the following payments; Veterans Affairs compensation and pension, education MGIB, education/selected reserve, life insurance and vocational rehabilitation and employment benefits; and Civil Service retirement and survivor annuity.

Service

Using the ACH entry class code ENR is an enrollment process that allows financial institutions to use the ACH to begin Direct Deposit payments fast. Enrollments received and accepted by the paying agency at least 10 business days prior to the customer's next scheduled payment date will generally allow the recipient's next month's payment by Direct Deposit.

A unique Standard Entry Class Code, Automated Enrollment (ENR) is used for enrollments where customers are converting their payment from paper check to direct deposit. ENR is not to be used to transfer existing direct deposit enrollments from one financial institution to another or changing an existing direct deposit relationship between accounts at the current institution.

The ENR Standard Entry Class is a non-dollar transaction. It must contain at least one addenda record, and may contain as many as 9,999 addenda records. There are two conditions that must exist for multiple addenda to be included with one ENR.

1. All Direct Deposit enrollments must be for the same Federal agency benefit program. For example, do not mix enrollments for Veterans benefits with Social Security benefits.

2. Third-party processors that transmit ENR entries on behalf of financial institutions must make a discrete batch transmission for each financial institution. Addenda records pertaining to one financial institution should not be included under the same ENR entry as addenda records pertaining to another financial institution's Direct Deposit enrollments.

The ENR is to be used for enrolling payment recipients who currently receive paper checks in the Direct Deposit Program. It is not to be used in place of the Notification of Change (NOC) process to change the routing or account numbers for existing records. Financial institutions should remind customers of the importance of reporting address changes to the benefit program agency.

Required Enrollment Information

The following information is required to effect the enrollment of a recipient in Direct Deposit using the entry class code ENR. This information will be transmitted in the entry detail and the addenda record of an ENR transaction. This page may be duplicated and used for data collection. DO NOT mail this sheet to the agency. All information collected must refer to the individual who receives the federal benefit payment.

Information obtained from the customer (payment recipient) for inclusion in the entry detail record.

Type of payment: _____
(Social Security; SSI; Veterans compensation and pension, education MGIB, education/ selected reserve, life insurance and vocational rehabilitation and employment benefits; Civil Service retirement and survivor annuity; Railroad Retirement annuity and unemployment/sickness)

Information obtained from the customer regarding the payment recipient for inclusion in the Addenda record.

Benefit Recipient's social security number (SSN)   **SSN** _ _ _ _ _ _ _ _ _
(Do not include hyphens in the addenda record.)

The recipient's own SSN may or nay not be the SSN on which the benefits are drawn. However, the individual recipient's SSN will always be included on the addenda record. In cases such as minor children the SSN will always be the CHILD's SSN and not that of the adult account holder named on the financial institution's records.

Benefit Recipient's Name

_   _ _ _ _ _ _ _ _ _ _ _ _

Last name (up to 15 positions)   *First Name (up to 7 positions)*

Last name: This is the recipient's last name excluding any suffixes such as Jr., Sr. II, III, etc. . . If the last name is hyphenated, the fully hyphenated name up to 17 characters is submitted.

If the last name is comprised of two or more 'parts', generally, the first part is sent as the last name (i.e. MaryJane S Public Doe) The last name would be submitted as "PUBLIC" and the Doe would be excluded.

First name: This is the recipient's first name excluding any prefixes such as Dr., Mrs., Miss, etc. . .

Middle initials are not submitted in this field. Middle initials are dropped. However, fully spelt out middle names are included as part of the first name (i.e. Mary J Doe would be submitted as Mary, whereas, Mary Jane Doe would be submitted as Mary Jane.)

The 'parsed' name will always be submitted exactly as the parsed section appears on the recipient's benefit check. Therefore, incorrectly spelt or spaced items will be submitted as they appear on the check and not as they should be legally spelt. Example: Janie Ann Doe is trying to enroll; however, her check is printed Jane E A Doe. The enrollment would be submitted as "Jane" and "Doe".

Representative Payee indication   NO __ (0)(Zero)   Yes __ (1)
(See section on Representative Payee, page 1-38.)

Information obtained at the financial institution.

Depository Financial Institution routing number   RTN _ _ _ _ _ _ _ _   Check Digit __

Depositor Account Number   _ _ _ _ _ _ _ _ _ _ _ _ _ _ _ _ _
(Up to 17 positions)

Transaction Type: _____ **Checking** *(Type Code 22)* _____ **Savings** *(Type Code 32)*

For questions about submitting ENRs for a specific benefit payment, please call the corresponding Federal program agency:	Federal Agency	Telephone No.
	Social Security Administration (for SSA and SSI payments).....................................	(215) 597-1134
	Office of Personnel Management............................	(202) 606-0540
	Railroad Retirement Board..	(312) 751-4704
	Department of Veterans Affairs................................	(918) 687-2532

ENR (Automated Enrollment) Entry Detail Record

Field	1	2	3	4	5	6	7	8	9	10	11	12	13
Data Element Name	Record Type Code	Transaction Code	Receiving DFI Identification	Check Digit	DFI Account Number	Amount	Identification Number	No. of Addenda Records	Receiving Company Name/ID	Reserved	Discretionary Data	Addenda Record Indicator	Trace Number
Field Incursion Requirement	M	M	M	M	R	M	O	M	R	N/A	O	M	M
Contents	'6'	(numeric)*			(blanks)	(all zeros)	(blanks)	(numeric)		(blanks)	(blanks)	(numeric)	(numeric)
Length	1	2	8	1	17	10	15	4	16	2	2	1	15
Position	01-01	02-03	04-11	12-12	13-29	30-39	40-54	55-58	59-74	76-76	77-78	79-79	80-94

*use either 23 or 33 in Field 2

Program Payment	Field 3 Receiving DFI Identification	Field 4 Check Digit	Field 9 Receiving Company Name/ID
The following program payments are eligible for the enrollment service	Use the following DFI Identification number for the corresponding program payment	Use the following number for the corresponding program payment	Use the following codes for the corresponding program for which the recipient is enrolling for Direct Deposit
Social Security	65506004	2	SOCIALbSECURITYb
Supplemental Social Security	65506004	2	SUPPbSECURITYbbb
Veterans Compensation and Pension	11173699	1	VAbCOMP/PENSION
Veterans Education MGIB	11173699	1	VAbEDUCATNbMGIB
Veterans Education/Selected Reserve	11173699	1	VAbECUDbMGIB/SR
Veterans Life Insurance	11173699	1	VAbLIFEbINSUR
Veterans Vocational Rehabilitation and Employment Benefits	11173699	1	VAbVOCbREHABbEMP
Civil Service Retirement/Annuity	11173699	1	CIVILbSERVbCSAbb
Civil Service Survivor/Annuity	11173699	1	CIVILbSERVbCSFbb
Railroad Retirement Annuity	11173699 (*)	1 (*)	RAILROADbRETbBDb
Railroad Unemployment/Sickness	11173699 (*)	1 (*)	RAILROADbUISIbbb
Dependents Education Assistance Program	11173699	1	VAbDEPbEDUbASST
Reserve Education Assistance Program	11173699	1	VAbEDUCTNbREAP
Post 911 GI Bill	11173699	1	VAbEDUbPOSTb9/11

NOTE: In the codes, the letter "b" indicates a blank space

ENR Addenda Record

Field	1	2	3	4	5
Data Element Name	Record Type Code	Addenda Type Code	Payment Related Information	Addenda Sequence Number	Entry Detail Sequence Number
Field Inclusion Requirement	M	M	R	M	M
Contents	'7'	'05'	'22*12200004*3*123987654321*777777777*DOE*JOHN*0\'	(numeric)	(numeric)
Length	1	2	80	4	7
Position	01-01	02-03	04-83	84-87	88-94

Field 3 - Payment Related Information									
The following uses sample information to illustrate the required information to be included in the Addenda record to effect the automated enrollment for Direct Deposit. The standard for submission of ENR records is for all alphabetic characters anywhere in the file to be submitted in UPPER CASE. Failure to do so may result in the submission to be returned by the paying agency. Refer to page 1-38 Return Reasons Codes.									
22 = Checking Account 32 = Savings Account	*	12200004	3	123987654321	777777777	DOE	JOHN	0= No Rep. Payee 1= Rep. Payee	\
Contents	Delimiter	'05'	Check Digit	Receiver's Acct. No. at the Financial Institution (up to 17 positions)	Receiver's Own Social Security No.	Receiver's Surname (up to 15)	Receiver's First Name (up to 7)	Representative Payee Indicator	Terminator

Representative Payee

A representative payee is a person or institution that is legally entitled to receive payments on behalf of a beneficiary who has been deemed incapable of handling his/her own financial affairs. The majority of benefit recipients do not have representative payees. When a representative payee is present, both names will appear on the benefit check. Minor children receiving federal benefits should always have a representative payee. Some examples of representative check payee styles are:

Mary Smith for Jane R. Doe
Harry D. Doe, Guardian for John Q. Public
Admin Sunnyvale Nursing Home for Mary T. Resident

Questions regarding the styling of representative payee names by a particular agency should be directed to that specific agency.

In processing an enrollment, it is important for the processing financial institution and enrolling benefit agency to know that the enrollment originated from the proper authority. In cases where there is a representative payee, a "1" will be entered as the last data element in Field 3 of the addenda. In instances where there is no representative payee, a "0" (zero) will be entered into this position.

The Federal Government requires that the title of accounts receiving Direct Deposit payments bear the name of the payment recipient. Accounts established for representative payee payments reflect fiduciary interest of the representative payee on behalf of the beneficiary. (Example of an account title: John Doe for Mary Smith.) This same regulation applies to institutional representative payees. **The Depart of Veterans Affairs and the Office of Personnel Management do not allow ENR enrollments for representative payees.**

Return Reason Codes

If it is necessary for a Federal agency to return an ENR entry to the financial institution as unprocessable, one of the following codes will be indicated on the return:

R40 Non-Participant in ENR Program - The Federal program agency is not a participant in the ENR automated enrollment program.

R41 Invalid Transaction Code - An incorrect or inappropriate transaction code is used in Field 3 of the Addenda record.

R42 Routing Number/Check Digit Error - The Routing Number and/or the Check Digit included in Field 3 of the Addenda record is incorrect.

R43 Invalid DFI Account Number - The receiver's account number at the DFI is either missing, exceeds 17 positions, or contains invalid characters.

R44 Invalid Individual ID Number - The receiver's SSN provided in Field 3 of the Addenda record does not match a corresponding SSN in the benefit agency's records.

R45 Invalid Individual Name - The name of the receiver provided in Field 3 of the Addenda record either does not match a corresponding name in the benefit agency's records <u>or</u> fails to include at least one alphanumeric character.

R46 Invalid Representative Payee Indicator - The representative payee indicator code included in Field 3 of the Addenda record has been omitted <u>or</u> it is not consistent with the benefit agency's records

R47 Duplicate Enrollment - The Federal agency has received duplicate Automated Enrollment entries from the same DFI

For more complete information concerning return reason codes and their interpretation, refer to the *National Automated Clearing House Association ACH Operating Rules*.

Note: At least one paying agency requires that any alphabetic data in an ENR record must be submitted in all UPPER CASE. Therefore, the de facto standard for submission of ENR records is for all alphabetic characters located anywhere in the file to be submitted in UPPER CASE. Failure to do so may result in the submission to be returned as an R44/R45 item even though all the information is correct.

ENR Tips and Information Checklist

General Questions / Information:

1. Are you currently receiving Direct Deposit?
   - If yes, then you will need to contact your paying agency to change any existing banking information.
     - The Social Security Administration   1-800-722-1213
     - The Office of Personnel Management   1-800-767-6738
     - The Railroad Retirement Board   1-800-808-0772
   - If no, do you have or have you opened a checking or savings account?

2. If you are unable to open a regular checking or savings account and are interested in an Electronic Transfer Account (ETA), you can call toll free 1-888-382-3311. A representative would be happy to assist you in finding a bank that offers an ETA account (a low cost account).

3. The benefit recipient or representative payee must be present in order to sign up for direct deposit in person. If by phone, the recipient or representative payee must be present to give permission.

4. Is the federal benefit check in the customer's name only? If no, determine whether there is a representative payee relationship or not.

Benefit Recipient Information

5. Benefit recipient - the person who receives the federal benefit payment

6. Representative payee - the benefit comes in their name or on behalf of someone else.

7. "In C/O" - the benefit comes to the benefit recipient "in care of" someone else. That does not mean the person the check is in care of is the representative payee. The benefit recipient must be present to enroll.

8. If the customer has Power of Attorney for the benefit recipient, they must go to the local office of the paying agency to sign up for direct deposit. If the benefit recipient is not present, the customer will need to take all legal documents with them to a regional office of the paying agency. The paying agency does not accept enrollments based solely on a Power of Attorney.

9. If the customer is the guardian of the benefit recipient and his/her name is on the benefit check as guardian for the benefit recipient, then the F.I. would treat them as a representative payee. If his/her name is not on the benefit check he/she must go to the local paying agency office with all legal documents.

Information Needed for Direct Deposit Enrollment

The following information is needed to enroll SSA/SSI, RRB, and OPM payments for direct deposit through the U.S. Treasury's Go Direct program.

10. The social security number of the benefit recipient. This is always the individual benefit recipient's SSN. This is never the representative payee's or anyone else's SSN.

11. The routing and account number of the checking or savings account.

If Enrolling through the Go Direct Call Center or via FMS Form 1200

12. The benefit recipient's claim number or check number of the most recent federal benefit check received and the payment amount.

- The claim number can be located on any correspondence the benefit recipient has received from the paying agency. If it is a Social Security payment, the claim number can be found on the Medicare Card if applicable.

- If the payment is Supplemental Security Income (SSI), the claim number is the benefit recipient's social security number.

- If the payment is Railroad Retirement, we need the most recent check number - the claim number will not process.

- If the payment is Civil Service (Office of Personnel Management), we need the most recent check number - the claim number will not process.

13. The federal benefit check numbers are located in the top right hand corner of the federal benefit check. The check numbers are 12 digits long. It will start with 4 digits then a space and 8 more digits. All 12 numbers must be entered with no spaces and no dashes.

14. The claim number must be entered with no spaces or dashes. All numbers and letters must be entered side by side.

Payment Type

15. If the customer normally receives a payment on the 1st day of the month, it is either a SSI payment, a civil service payment, or a railroad retirement payment.

16. If the customer normally receives a payment on the 3rd day of the month, the 2nd, 3rd or 4th Wednesday, it is a social security payment.

17. If the customer has their benefit check in hand, payment type is printed to the left of the dollar amount on the check.

18. If benefit checks come in blue envelopes they are Supplemental Security Income (SSI) payments.

Helpful Numbers and Web Sites

19. For SSA/SSI, RRB, and OPM enrollments please enroll through either:

Go Direct web enrollment: *http://www.godirect.org*

U.S. Treasury Electronic Payment Solutions Center
1-800-333-1795 (English) / 1-800-333-1792 (Spanish)
8:00 am – 8:00 pm ET, Monday – Friday, excluding Federal Holidays.

20. Department of Defense (DOD) or Black Lung payments can not be set up through ENR.
Contact Information:
- Veterans Affairs   1-800-827-1000
- DOD   *www.mypay.gov*
- Black Lung   *http://www.dol.gov/esa/contacts/owep/blcontac.htm*

Paperwork Reduction Act Statement

This information collection meets the requirements of 44 U.S.C. § 3507, as amended by section 2 of the Paperwork Reduction Act of 1995. You do not need to answer these questions unless we display a valid Office of Management and Budget control number. The OMB control number for this collection is 0960-0564. We estimate that it will take about 3 minutes to read the instructions, gather the facts, and answer the questions. You may send comments on our time estimate above to: SSA, 1338 Annex Building, Baltimore, MD 21235-0001. Send only comments relating to our time estimate to this address, not the completed form.

Federal Agency Addresses and Phone Numbers

These are the Federal agency addresses where you should send the completed SF 1199A, and/or telephone numbers if you need assistance. If a telephone number is not listed and further assistance is needed, please contact the Financial Management Service Customer Assistance Staff in your region.

Note: *As with any listing of this type, contact information will frequently change. Should you find out-of-date information, please let us know by email at: greenbook@fms.treas.gov.*

Air Force	**Active Duty / Reserves** Recipient should deliver the completed SF 1199A to his/her payroll office. Questions: (303) 676-7213 **Air National Guard** Recipient should deliver the completed SF 1199A to his/her payroll office. **Retirement / Annuity** DFAS-CL U.S. Military Retirement and Annuitant Pay 1240 E. Ninth Street Cleveland, Ohio 44199-2055 Retirement / Annuity: 1 (800) 321-1080 Allotments: (216) 522-5553
Army	**Active Duty / Reserves / National Guard** Recipient must mail or deliver the completed SF 1199A to his/her payroll office. Questions: (317) 510-2800 **Retirement / Annuity** DFAS-CL U.S. Military Retirement and Annuitant Pay 1240 E. Ninth Street Cleveland, Ohio 44199-205 Retirement / Annuity: 1 (800) 321-1080

Bureau of the Fiscal Service	**Federal Housing Administration Debenture Payments** Special Investments Branch P/O. Box 396 Parkersburg, WV 26106-0396 Questions: (304) 480-5299 **Savings Bond Agent's Fee Payments** Bureau of the Fiscal Service Accounts and Reports Section Parkersburg, WV 26106-1328 Questions: 1-800-722-2678 **Series H / HH Savings Bond Interest Payments** Bureau of the Fiscal Service Current Income Bond Branch Parkersburg, WV 26106-1328 Questions: (304) 480-6112 **State and Local Government Payments** Bureau of the Fiscal Service State and Local Government Payments Parkersburg, WV 26106-1328 Questions: (304) 480-5299
Central Intelligence Agency	Send completed forms to... Central Intelligence Agency Washington, DC 20505 Attn: Compensation Division Office of Finance
Coast Guard	**Active Duty / Reserves** Mail or have the recipient deliver the completed SF 1199A form to his/her payroll office. **Retirement** Coast Guard (RPD) Commanding Officers USGC-PPC Pay and Personnel Office 444 SE Quincy Street Topeka, KS 66683

Department of Labor	**Black Lung**	Send all completed SF 1199As to the district offices listed below.

Questions?
Call toll-free: 1-800-638-7072 or see the
Department of Labor website:
www.dol.gov/esa/regs/compliance/owcp/bltable.htm
or contact your district office listed below

Johnstown, PA

U.S. Department of Labor
ESA / OWCP / DCMWC
319 Washington Street, 2nd Floor
Johnstown, PA 15901
(800) 347-3754
(814) 533-4323

Greensburg, PA

U.S. Department of Labor
ESA / OWCP / DCMWC
1225 S. Main Street, Suite 405
Greensburg, PA 15601
(800) 347-3753
(724) 836-7230

Wilkes-Barre, PA

U.S. Department of Labor
ESA / OWCP / DCMWC
100 N. Wilkes-Barre Blvd.
Room 300 A
Wilkes-Barre, PA 187002
(800) 347-3755
(570) 826-6457

Charleston, WV

U.S. Department of Labor
ESA / OWCP / DCMWC
Charleston Federal Center, Suite 110
500 Quarrier Street
Charleston, WV 25301
(800) 347-3749
(304) 347-7100

Parkersburg, WV

U.S. Department of Labor
ESA / OWCP / DCMWC
425 Juliana Street, Suite 3116
Parkersburg, WV 26101
(800) 347-3751
(304) 420-6385

Department of Labor — Black Lung (continued)	Pikeville, KY	U.S. Department of Labor ESA / OWCP / DCMWC 164 Main Street, Suite 508 Pikeville, KY 41501 (800) 366-4599 (606) 432-0116
	Mount Sterling, KY	U.S. Department of Labor ESA / OWCP / DCMWC 402 Campbell Way Mount Sterling, KY 40353 (800) 366-4628 (859) 498-9700
	Columbus, OH	U.S. Department of Labor ESA / OWCP / DCMWC 1160 Dublin Road, Suite 300 Columbus, OH 43215 (800) 347-3771 (614) 469-5227
	Denver, CO	U.S. Department of Labor ESA / OWCP / DCMWC 1999 Broadway, Suite 690 P.O. Box 46550 Denver, CO 80201-6550 (800) 366-4612 (720) 264-3100

If the district office is unknown, mail the completed SF 1199A form to:
U.S. Department of Labor
Black Lung Program
P.O. Box 37227
Washington, DC 20013

Department of Labor	**Federal Employee Workers' Compensation**	Send all completed SF 1199As to ... U.S. Department of Labor Division of Federal Employees' Compensation Central Mail Room P.O. Box 8300 London, KY 40742

Questions? See the Department of Labor website: *www.dol.gov/esa/contacts/owcp/fecacont.htm* or contact your district office located below.

Department of Labor — FEWC (continued)	BOSTON District 1	For CT, ME, MA, NH, RI, VT (617) 624-6600
	NEW YORK District 2	For NJ, NY, PR, VI (646) 264-3000
	PHILADELPHIA District 3	For DE, PA, WV (215) 861-5481*, 5482 * The Interactive Voice Response System can also be accessed from this number.
	JACKSONVILLE District 6	For AL, FL, GA, KY, MS, NC, SC, TN (904) 357-4777*, 4778 * The Interactive Voice Response System can also be accessed from this number.
	CLEVELAND District 9	For IN, MI, OH (216) 357-5100
	CHICAGO District 10	For IL, MN, WI (312) 596-7157* * The Interactive Voice Response System can also be accessed from this number
	KANSAS CITY District 11	For IA< MO< NE; DOL employees (816) 502-0301
	DENVER District 12	For CO, MT, ND, SD, UT, WY (720) 264-3000* * The Interactive Voice Response System can also be accessed from this number.
	SAN FRANCISCO District 13	For AZ, CA, HI, NV (415) 848-6700
	SEATTLE District 14	For AK, ID, OR, WA (206) 398-8100
	DALLAS District 16	For AR, LA, NM, OK, TX (972) 850-2300
	WASHINGTON, DC District 25	For DC, MD, VA; outside U.S. and its possessions; special claims (202) 513-6800* * The Interactive Voice Response System can also be accessed from this number.

Department of Labor	Longshore and Harbor Workers' Compensation	Send all completed SF 1199As to ... U.S. Department of Labor ESA / OWCP / DLHWC Frances Perkins Building Room C4315 200 Constitution Avenue, NW Washington, DC 20210 Questions: (202) 693-0925
Department of Veterans Affairs		Mail the completed SF 1199A form to the office that maintains the veteran's records
	ALABAMA	Alabama VA Regional Office 345 Perry Hill Road Montgomery, AL 36104 Questions: 1 (800) 827-1000
	ALASKA	Anchorage VA Regional Office 2925 DeBarr Road Anchorage, AK 99508-2989
	ARIZONA	Arizona VA Regional Office 3225 N. Central Avenue Phoenix, AZ 85012
	ARKANSAS	North Little Rock VA Regional Office 345 Perry Hill Road Montgomery, AL 36104
	CALIFORNIA	Los Angeles VA Regional Office Federal Building 1100 Wilshire Boulevard Los Angeles, CA 90024 San Diego VA Regional Office 8810 Rio San Diego Drive San Diego, CA 92018 Oakland VA Regional Office Oakland Federal Building 1301 Clay Street, Room 1300N Oakland, CA 94612

Department of Veterans Affairs (continued)	COLORADO	Denver VA Regional Office 155 Van Gordon Street Lakewood, CO 80228
	CONNECTICUT	Hartford VA Regional Office 450 Main Street Hartford, CT 06103
	DELAWARE	Wilmington VA Regional Office 1601 Kirkwood Highway Wilmington, DE 19805
	DISTRICT OF COLUMBIA	Washington DC VA Regional Office 1120 Vermont Avenue, NW Washington, DC 20421
	FLORIDA	St. Petersburg VA Regional Office 9500 Bay Pines Boulevard Bay Pines, FL 33708
	GEORGIA	Atlanta VA Regional Office 1700 Clairmont Road Decatur, GA 30033
	HAWAII	Honolulu VA Regional Office 459 Patterson Road, E-Wing Honolulu, HI 96819-1522
	IDAHO	Boise VA Regional Office 805 W. Franklin Street Boise, ID 83702
	ILLINOIS	Chicago VA Regional Office 536 S. Clark Street Chicago, IL 60605-1523
	INDIANA	Indianapolis VA Regional Office 75 NB. Pennsylvania Street Indianapolis, IN 46204 Questions: (317) 226-7860
	IOWA	Des Moines VA Regional Office 210 Walnut Street Des Moines, IA 50309

Department of Veterans Affairs (continued)	KANSAS	Wichita VA Regional Office 5500 E. Kellogg Wichita, KS 67211
	KENTUCKY	Louisville VA Regional Office 545 S. Third Street Louisville, KY 40202
	LOUISIANA	New Orleans VA Regional Office 701 Loyola Avenue New Orleans, LA 70113
	MAINE	Togus Center One VA Center Togus, ME 04330
	MARYLAND	Baltimore VA Regional Office 31 Hopkins PLaza Baltimore, MD 21201
	MASSACHUSETTS	Boston VA Regional Office John Fitzgerald Kennedy Federal Building Government Center Boston, MA 02114
	MICHIGAN	Detroit VA Regional Office Patrick V. McNamara Federal Building 477 Michigan Avenue Detroit, MI 48226
	MINNESOTA	St. Paul VA Regional Office One Federal Drive, Fort Snelling St. Paul, MN 55111-4050
	MISSISSIPPI	Jackson VA Regional Office 1600 E. Woodrow Wilson Avenue Jackson, MS 39216
	MISSOURI	St. Louis VA Regional Office Federal Building 400 S. 18th Street St. Louis, MO 63103

Department of Veterans Affairs (continued)	MONTANA	Fort Harrison Medical & Regional Center William Street off Highway Fort Harrison, MT 59636
	NEBRASKA	Lincoln VA Regional Office 5631 S. 48th Street Lincoln, NE 68516
	NEVADA	Reno VA Regional Office 1201 Terminal Way Reno, NV 89520
	NEW HAMPSHIRE	Manchester VA Regional Office Norris Cotton Federal Building 275 Chestnut Street Manchester, NH 03101
	NEW JERSEY	New Jersey VA Regional Office 20 Washington Place Newark, NJ 07102
	NEW MEXICO	Albuquerque VA Regional Office Davis Chavez Federal Building 500 Gold Avenue, SW Albuquerque, NM 87102
	NEW YORK	Buffalo VA Regional Office Federal Building 111 W. Hurron Street Buffalo, NY 14202
		New York VA Regional Office 245 W. Houston Street New York, NY 10014
	NORTH CAROLINA	Winston-Salem VA Regional Office Federal Building 251 N. Main Street Winston-Salem, NC 27155
	NORTH DAKOTA	Fargo VA Medical / Regional Office Center 2101 Elm Street Fargo, ND 58102 Questions: (701) 232-3421

Department of Veterans Affairs (continued)	OHIO	Cleveland VA Regional Office Anthony J. Celebrezze Federal Building 1240 E. Ninth Street Cleveland, OH 44119
	OKLAHOMA	Muskogee VA Regional Office Federal Building 125 S. Main Street Muskogee, OK 74401
	OREGON	Portland VA Regional Office Federal Building 1220 SW 3rd Avenue Portland, OR 97204 Questions: (503) 326-2511
	PENNSYLVANIA	Philadelphia VA Center 5000 Wissahickon Avenue Philadelphia, PA 19101
		Pittsburgh VA Regional Office 1000 Liberty Avenue Pittsburgh, PA 15222
	RHODE ISLAND	Providence VA Regional Office 380 Westminster Mall Westminster, RI 02903
	SOUTH CAROLINA	Columbia VA Regional Office 1801 Assembly Street Columbia, SC 29201
	SOUTH DAKOTA	Sioux Falls VA Center P.O. Box 5046 2501 W. 22nd Street Sioux Falls, SD 57117
	TENNESSEE	Nashville VA Regional Office 110 9th Avenue, South Nashville, TN 37203
	TEXAS	Houston VA Regional Office 6900 Almeda Road Houston, TX 77030

Department of Veterans Affairs (continued)	TEXAS	Waco VA Regional Office One Veterans Plaza 701 Clay Avenue Waco, TX 76799
	UTAH	Salt Lake City VA Regional Office 550 Foothill Drive Salt Lake City, UT 84158
	VERMONT	White River Junction VA Medical & Regional Office Center 215 N. Main Street White River Junction, VT 05009
	WASHINGTON	Seattle VA Regional Office Federal Building 915 Second Avenue Seattle, WA 98174
	WEST VIRGINIA	Huntington VA Regional Office 640 Fourth Avenue Huntington, WV 25701
	WISCONSIN	Milwaukee VA Regional Office 5000 W. National Avenue Milwaukee, WI 53295
	WYOMING	Cheyenne VA Medical / Regional Center 2360 E. Pershing Boulevard Cheyenne, WY 82001
	GUAM	Guam Vet Center 222 Chanlan Santo Papast Reflection Center, Suite 102 Agana, GU 96910 Questions: (705) 475-7161
	PHILIPPINES	Manila Regional Office 1131 Roxas Boulevard, Ermita 0930 Manila, PL 96440 Questions: (011) (632) 528-2500
	PUERTO RICO	San Juan VA Center 150 Carlos Chardon Avenue Hato Rey, PR 00918

Department of Veterans Affairs (continued)	VIRGIN ISLANDS	St. Croix Vet Center Box 12, R.R. 02, Village Mail, #113Affairs Saint Croix, VI 00850 Questions: 1 (809) 778-5553 Saint Thomas Vet Center Buccaneer Mall Saint Thomas, VI 00801 Questions: 1 (809) 774-6674
Federal Salary		The employee should mail or deliver the completed SF 1199A form to his / her payroll office.
Marine Corps		**Active Duty / Reserves** Director DFAS – Kansas City Center (AF-FA) Kansas City, MO 64197-0001 Questions: (303) 676-7213 **Retirement / Annuity** DFAS – CL U.S. Military Retirement and Annuitant Pay 1240 E. Ninth Street Cleveland, OH 44199-2055 Questions: 1 (800) 321-1080
Navy		**Active Duty / Reserves** Mail or have the recipient deliver the completed SF 1199A form to his / her payroll office Questions: 1 (800) 255-0974 **Retirement / Annuity** DFAS – CL U.S. Military Retirement and Annuitant Pay 1240 E. Ninth Street Cleveland, OH 44199-2055 Questions: 1 (800) 321-1080
Office of Personnel Management (Civil Service Annuity)		Send completed forms to . . . Office of Personnel Management Change-of-address Section-ROC Retirement and Insurance Group P.O. Box 440 Boyers, PA 16017-0440 Questions: (202) 606-0500

Railroad Retirement Board

Send completed forms to . . .

- the local Railroad Retirement Board as listed in the telephone directory; or,
- if you cannot obtain the address of the local office, mail to:

  U.S. Railroad Retirement Board
  P.O. Box 10792
  844 N. Rush Street
  Chicago, IL 60611
  Attn: Direct Deposit Coordinator ORSP
  Questions (312) 751-4500 or (312) 751-4707

Social Security Administration

Send completed forms to . . .

- the local Social Security District Office; or,
- the address Social Security has specified to your financial institution.

G. Automated Standard Application for Payments (ASAP)

General Information

The Automated Standard Application for Payments (ASAP) system is a recipient-initiated payment and information system, designed to provide a single point of contact for the request and delivery of Federal funds. ASAP provides timely delivery of Federal funds to coincide with the outlays of recipient organizations to meet program needs.

A payment requester in ASAP is an organization authorized to draw Federal funds for use by one or more recipient organizations. In some instances a recipient organization has the authority to draw its own Federal funds, in which case that organization is both a payment requester and a recipient organization in ASAP.

Federal agencies, payment requesters, and recipient organizations enroll one time to use ASAP. Federal agencies establish and maintain accounts in ASAP to control the flow of funds to recipient organizations. Payment requesters initiate payment requests via ASAP to meet the cash needs of recipient organizations. Approved requests are paid either the same day via the Federal Reserve's Fedwire System or on a date up to 32 days from the request date via the Federal Reserve's Automated Clearing House (ACH) system.

Financial Institution Role

The financial institution plays a key role in the ASAP program by providing the financial institution link between ASAP and the payment requester / recipient organization. Financial institutions must provide the payment related information contained in the addenda to the recipient organization in compliance with NACHA Operating Rules. It is important that the financial institution work closely with the payment requester / recipient organization.

The ASAP Payment Requester Bank Information Form is used to specify the financial institution and account number to which ASAP payments are to be directed. The customer may request the financial institution to verify banking information, including the ABA and account number. Upon receipt of the form, the Government Disbursing Office will only issue a prenote prior to processing any drawdown requests. For more information, please contact the FMS Customer Assistance Staff (See Chapter 8, Contacts).

H. Termination of Enrollment

The ACH Enrollment authorization may be revoked by the recipient or, under certain circumstances, by the financial institution.

Termination by the Recipient

The recipient may revoke the enrollment authorization at any time by notifying the Federal agency, or by authorizing a new enrollment with another financial institution.

Social Security or Supplemental Security Income recipients should call **1 (800) SSA-1213** or write their local Social Security District Office to revoke the enrollment authorization.

Railroad Retirement Board annuitants may either write or call the local Railroad Retirement Board Field Office to revoke the enrollment authorization.

Series H / HH savings bond owners who are required to receive interest payments by Direct Deposit may revoke the enrollment authorization. However, this will result in suspension of payments. Payments will resume when the recipient authorizes a new enrollment.

OPM Annuitants may either write or call **1 (888) 767-6738** to revoke the enrollment authorization. They may also visit *www.opm.gov/retire* to terminate and make changes on-line.

The enrollment authorization will be terminated due to the recipient's or beneficiary's death or legal incapacity.

Courtesy Notice

The recipient or beneficiary is not required to inform the financial institution if he / she revokes or transfers his / her enrollment authorization. As a courtesy, the recipient should be encouraged to inform the financial institution of any changes.

Termination by the Financial Institution

Financial institutions may close an account to which benefit payments are currently being sent thereby revoking the enrollment authorization by providing a 30-day written notice to the recipient prior to closing the account. In cases involving fraud, accounts may be closed immediately. The financial institution cannot revoke the enrollment authorization by notifying the Federal agency and not the recipient.

The 30-day written notice should remind the recipient to make other arrangements for the handling of his / her payments. The financial institution must credit to the recipient's account any payments received during the 30-day notice period. The financial institution must also immediately return to the Federal government all payments received after the 30-day notice period. A financial institution that closes the account without properly termination the enrollment must make the funds available to the recipient until proper notice is provided.

Receipt Notice to the Federal Agency

The recipient or beneficiary must immediately advise the Federal agency if the enrollment authorization is revoked by the financial institution.

2 ACH Payment Processing

Overview

This chapter provides information about how Federal government ACH payments are processed. It also contains valuable information on payment dates and information to assist in identifying Treasury disbursed payments.

In this Chapter...

A. Financial Organization Master File (FOMF)

The Financial Organization Master File (FOMF) is a Department of the Treasury master list of financial institutions receiving Federal government Automated Clearing House (ACH) payments. It contains Routing Numbers (RTN) and a single financial institution name and mailing address for each RTN.

The FOMF is derived from the Federal Reserve Bank's (FRB's) ACH Customer Directory (ACD), which contains the RTNs and related information of all valid ACH participants. The FOMF is updated on a monthly basis using information from the most current ACD file.

Purpose

The Financial Management Service (FMS) relies on the FOMF data to validate RTNs used to originate payments and to send financial institutions the following:

- reclamation notices
- trace inquiries
- marketing materials

Financial Institution Responsibility

Changes to Financial Institution Name and Mailing Address

Financial institutions are responsible for keeping their name and mailing address for each RTN up to date with the FRB. Any changes to RTN data should be provided to the FRB as soon as possible so that the ACD and FOMF contain current data. If the financial institution fails to notify the FRB, it may be held liable for information (e.g., reclamation notices) mailed to obsolete addresses.

Changes to Routing Numbers

If a financial institution changes RTNs (e.g., due to merger), it must notify its servicing FRB's ACH Department as soon as possible to have the old RTN to have the ACH reflect the Financial Institution's active ACH routing numbers. Updates to the ACD will update the FOMF. Additionally, financial institutions should send a notification of change (NOC) to each originating Federal agency from which it receives payments affected by the routing number changes.

The following steps should be taken in updating the ACD routing number data:

- Confirm that no activity is being received on the obsolete RTN prior to deletion.
- Allow at least three months after the update to the ACD before deleting an obsolete RTN.
- Delete an obsolete RTN only after all activity has been transferred to the surviving RTN.

Updating ACD:

If an institution wants to update the information that appears on the file they should submit "Attachment E" of the FedACH Participation Agreement to their designated FedACH Central site. The FedACH Participation Agreement can be accessed on the FRB website: http://www.frbservices.org/StandardForms/index.html.

If you have any questions in reference to updating data, you should work with your Regional Payment Association or the appropriate FRB Central Operations Support Site:

Atlanta
Toll Free: (866) 234-5681

Minneapolis
Toll Free: (888) 883-2180

New Depository Institutions

Because the FOMF is updated on a monthly basis, a new depository institution may not receive government ACH transactions for up to 30 days after being entered into the Federal Reserve Bank's ACD.

B. Federal Government ACH Processing

General Flow

Federal government ACH payments are initiated by the authorizing Federal agency to a Government Disbursing Office. These include the FMS, Department of Defense Disbursing Offices, and the Bureau of the Fiscal Service (for TreasuryDirectpayments). The Federal Reserve is the Federal government's ACH Operator.

Prenotification

The Federal government prenotification process is handled in accordance with NACHA Operating Rules. Social Security originates prenotifications for Direct Deposit enrollments and changes.

Payment Formats

Federal government ACH payments are originated in the Prearranged Payment and Deposit (PPD) with or without addenda, Corporate Debit or Credit (CCD) with or without addenda, or Corporate Trade Exchange (CTX) formats. Refer to the NACHA Operating Rules for details on payment record formats.

Account Requirements

All Federal government benefit payment enrollments must be established for a deposit account at the financial institution that is in the name of the recipient or beneficiary with the following exceptions:

- Where an authorized payment agent (representative payee) has been selected. A representative payee is an individual or organization appointed by SSA to receive Social Security and/or SSI benefits for someone who cannot manage or direct someone else to manage his or her money. The main responsibilities of a payee are to use the benefits to pay for the current and foreseeable needs of the beneficiary and properly save any benefits not needed to meet current needs. A payee must also keep records of expenses.

- Where the payment is to be deposited into an investment account established through a securities broker or dealer registered with the Securities and Exchange Commission, or an investment account established through an investment company registered under the Investment Company Act of 1940 or its transfer agent. The payment may be deposited into an account designated by the broker or dealer, investment company, or transfer agent.

- Where a Federal payment is disbursed to a resident of a nursing facility, as defined in 42 U.S.C. 1396r, the payment may be deposited into a resident trust or patient fund account established by the nursing facility so long as it meets the requirements under Federal law relating to the protection of such funds. For more information on these requirements, please visit the ACH regulations website at http://www.fms.treas.gov/ach.

- Where a Federal payment is disbursed to a member of a religious order who has taken a vow of poverty, the payment may be deposited to an account established by the religious order. The phrase ``member of a religious order who has taken a vow of poverty'' is defined as it would be by the Internal Revenue Service for Federal tax purposes.

- Where a Federal payment is to be deposited to an account accessed by the recipient through a prepaid card that meets the following requirements:

  (A) The account is held at an insured financial institution;

  (B) The account is set up to meet the requirements for pass-through deposit or share insurance such that the funds accessible through the card are insured for the benefit of the recipient by the Federal Deposit Insurance Corporation or the National Credit Union Share Insurance Fund in accordance with applicable law (12 CFR part 330 or 12 CFR part 745);

  (C) The account is not attached to a line of credit or loan agreement under which repayment from the account is triggered upon delivery of the Federal payments; and

  (D) The issuer of the card complies with all of the requirements, and provides the holder of the card with all of the consumer protections, that apply to a payroll card account under the rules implementing the Electronic Fund Transfer Act, as amended.

  No person or entity may issue a prepaid card that receives Federal payments in violation of these requirements, and no financial institution may maintain an account for or on behalf of an issuer of a prepaid card that receives Federal payments if the issuer violates these requirements. If FMS becomes aware that a prepaid card product that accepts Federal government payments does not meet these requirements, it will research the card product and report any violations of these requirements to the institutions' primarily regulator.

- Where Treasury has granted a waiver.

Misdirected Payments

On rare occasions, a Federal ACH payment is misdirected to the incorrect account. If the payee's account number is different from what is contained in the ACH entry, but the FI can identify the correct receiver, the FI may post the payment to the correct account as long as there is no change in the title of the account or in the interest of the recipient or beneficiary in the account. The FI does this at its own risk and may be liable to the issuing agency if the FI is incorrect and there is a resulting loss by the agency. If the FI does post the payment to an account other than that identified in the transaction, then an appropriate NOC with the correct account number should be sent to the agency. Please see Chapter 6, NOCs, for more information. If the FI cannot credit the misdirected payment to the correct account, the FI may return the payment to the agency with an appropriate reason code. Please see Chapter 4, Returns, for more information.

It is important to note that an FI is not required to manually verify that the name on the ACH entry matches the name on the account at the time the payment is posted. An RDFI is only liable for posting the payment to the account in the ACH credit entry.

Notice of Misdirected Payment

In accordance with Code 31 CFR Part 210, an RDFI that becomes aware that an agency has misdirected an ACH credit entry to the wrong account must promptly notify the agency. A financial institution may become aware of a misdirected payment through the following ways:

- The account holder notifies the financial institution of the misdirected payment

- A non-receipt claim being investigated by FMS

- A financial institution that manually posts their ACH credits notices that a payment is being credited to the wrong account. (It is important to note that an institution is not required to match names when posting a Federal government ACH entry; however, if it routinely posts entries manually and notices that an entry is being directed to the wrong account, it is required to notify the agency.)

- A call from the Federal agency that disbursed the payment

If a financial institution becomes aware of a misdirected payment, it can notify the agency in the following ways and meet the requirements of 31 CFR Part 210:

- The RDFI decides to manually post the misdirected payment to the correct account and originates a Notification of Change (NOC) entry with the correct account and/or Routing and Transit Number information (Please note that the FI does this at its own risk and may be liable to the issuing agency if the FI is incorrect and there is a resulting loss by the agency.)

- Return the original ACH credit entry to the agency with the appropriate return reason code

- Contact the agency by phone or by letter. Please see Chapter 8, Contacts.

- Any other means deemed acceptable by the agency that disbursed the ACH credit payment

Availability of Funds

In accordance with NACHA Operating Rules, consumer payments (i.e., Federal salary and travel payments, benefit payments) must be made available for withdrawal no later than the opening of business on the settlement date (provided the entries are made available to the Receiving Depositary Financial Institution (RDFI) by its ACH operator no later than 5:00 p.m. on the business day prior to the settlement date). Corporate payments (i.e., vendor payments, non-benefit payments) must be made available for withdrawal on the settlement date.

Electronic Transfer Account (ETA^{SM})

The ETA is a low-cost account designed by Treasury to provide individuals who receive Federal benefit, wage, salary, or retirement payments the ability to receive their payments electronically. Any individual who receives a Federal benefit, wage, salary, or retirement payment is eligible to open an ETA. Financial institutions that choose to offer ETAs (ETA Providers) will enter into a Financial Agency Agreement with Treasury, outlining the duties of the financial institution.

C. Federal ACH Payment Schedule

FMS publishes the Federal ACH Payment Schedule annually in NACHA's "ACH Rules: A Complete Guide to Rules and Regulations Governing the ACH Network." This listing provides the actual payment date for recurring Federal payments. The payment date equals the ACH settlement date. This listing is also available for viewing/download on the FMS website: www.fms.treas.gov/greenbook/achpay.html.

D. Identifying Treasury Disbursed Payments

Treasury disbursed payments can be identified using information contained in the Company/Batch Header Record. The Regional Financial Center/Routing Number Table on pages 2-7 to 2-8 lists the appropriate information for each FMS RFC. You can identify a payment by locating the following information:

RFC Symbol Number

Field 3, Company Name, of the Company/Batch Header Record

Routing Number

Field 12, Originating DFI Identification, of the Company/Batch Header Record

Sample Company/Batch Header Record (with identifying information highlighted)

101 111111111 2222222222205141842F094101 FEDACH US TREASURY PAM
5220BEP1 TREAS **303** 3333333333 CCD MISC PAY05151212051524444444444000001

RFC Symbol Number: 310 (Kansas City RFC), 303 (Philadelphia RFC), and 312 (San Francisco RFC).

Note: A '2' in field 11 of the Company/Batch Header Record identifies the Originator as a Federal government entity or agency.

Questions? Contact the FMS Payment Management Call Center **(855) 868 - 0151.**

Regional Financial Center/Routing Number Table

The table below lists the specific payments distributed by the Regional Financial Centers (RFC).

RFC	Symbol	Class of Payment
Kansas City	310	SSA PMA (Adjustment)
Questions?		SSA CMA/Recurring
Contact the FMS		SSA CMA/Recurring
Payment Management		Federal Salary
Call Center:		Travel
(855) 868-0151		Thirst Savings Plan
		Annuity
		Annuity
		Vendor/Miscellaneous
		IDD
		SSI Monthly
		SSI Daily
		VA Benefit
		VA Retro (Adjustment)
		VA Public Law Chapt 31
		VA EDUCATION CHAPTER 30
		VA EDUC CHAP 1606
		VA SPINA BIFIDA/CHAPTER 18
		VA (RESERVED)
		VA (RESERVED)
		VA (RESERVED)
		VA (RESERVED)
		VA (RESERVED)
		Federal Salary
		Travel
		Vendor/Miscellaneous
		Prime Pay

Regional Financial Center/Routing Number Table (cont.)

RFC	Symbol	Class of Payment
Philadelphia Questions? Contact the FMS Payment Management Call Center: (855) 868-0151	303	SSA PMA (Adjustment) SSA CMA/Recurring SSA CMA/Recurring Federal Salary Vendor/Miscellaneous SSA (CMA Recurring/INT'L) SSA (PMA/INT'L) Branch II Payments SSA/CMA Recurring Cycling SSA/CMA Recurring Cycling SSA/CMA Recurring Cycling RRB Daily (Adjustment) RRB UISI RRB Monthly BPD Pensions VA INSURANCE (RESERVED)
San Francisco Questions? Contact the FMS Payment Management Call Center: (855) 868-0151	312	OPM Monthly OPM Daily (Adjustment) SSA PMA (Adjustment) SSA CMA (Recurring) Federal Salary Travel IRS IMF (Tax) Vendor/Miscellaneous

 Note: Current Month Accrual (CMA), Prior Month Accrual (PMA)

Consumer Payments

Consumer Payment Formats

Consumer payments are designated for deposit into an individual's account. They are identified by the Standard Entry Class Code (SEC) to be used for consumer entries which is found in the Company/Batch Header Record (Field 6) of the payment file data.

Standard Entry Class Code

The Prearranged Payment and Deposit (PPD) is the SEC code used for identifying Federal agency consumer payments. The payment entries may be accompanied by a PPD addenda record (PPD+) which further identifies the reason for the payment.

Social Security Use of Prearranged Payment and Deposit (PPD+)
For Direct Deposit of Representative Fee Payments and Direct Deposit
of Representative Payees/Organizational Representative Payees

The Social Security Administration (SSA) issues fee payments either by check or direct deposit to individuals who have represented Social Security claimants and/or act as a representative payee. SSA has begun to use the PPD+ format for ACH payments to representatives that include adequate payment-related information that can be passed onto them to identify and credit the payment to the correct person/account. The information is included in Field 3 of the Addenda Record (Payment Related Information) and is based on ANSI X12 (American National Standards Institute coding for Electronic Data Interchange) syntax.

FMS encourages receiving financial institutions to pass through to their account holders, as quickly as possible, pertinent information from both the Entry Detail Record and the Addenda Record when a payment is received. The representative needs this addenda information to reconcile their client account records. The method of providing this information to the account holder is at the discretion of the financial institution and its customer.

Payment Types

Types of payments that utilize the PPD standard entry class category include the following:
- benefit
- annuity
- travel
- salary
- allotment
- IRS tax refund
- Public Debt payments.

Identifying the Paying Agency/Payment Type for Treasury Disbursed Payments

Field 7 "Company Entry Description" (Company/Batch Header Record)

Paying Agency/Payment Type	Field 7 Contents
Bureau of the Fiscal Service/TreasuryDirect	
Federal Housing Administration Debenture Payments . . .	FHA/HUD_ _ _
Marketable Securities (Bills, Notes, and Bonds)	PAR_AMOUNT PAR_&_INT_ INTEREST_ _ REFUND_ _ _ _
Savings Bond Agent's Fee Payments	AGENT_FEES Series HHH
Savings Bond Interest Payments	H/HH_INTST State and Local
Government Series Security Payments	SLG_PAYMNT
Central Intelligence Agency	
CIA Annuity.	CIARDSANNU
Department of Veterans Affairs	
Compensation and Pension	VA_BENEFIT
Federal Salary	FED_SALARY
Federal Travel Payments	FED_TRAVEL
Office of Personnel Management	
Civil Service Retirement (Annuity)	CIVIL_SERV
Railroad Retirement Board	
Railroad Retirement/Annuity.	RR_RET_ _ _ _
Unemployment/Sickness	RR_UISI
Social Security Administration	
Social Security	SOC_SEC_ _ _
Supplemental Security Income.	SUPP_SEC_ _

Identifying the Payee for Treasury Disbursed Payments

Field 7 Contents (Entry Detail Record)

IF the payment type is . . .	THEN Field 7 (Individual ID field) contents identify the payee by...
Bureau of the Fiscal Service/TreasuryDirect	
Marketable Securities (Bills, Notes, and Bonds) . . .	Account Number
Central Intelligence Agency	
CIA Annuity	Individual's SSN Positions 1-6 of the agency location code
Federal Salary	Individual's SSN or Employee's Identification Number and agency location code
Federal Travel	Individual's SSN or Employee's Identification Number and agency location code
Office of Personnel Management	
Civil Service Retirement (Annuity)	CSA (Annuitant) or CSF (Fiduciary) Blank Claim Number Prefix = A or F (most common) Claim Number (7 digit #) Claim Suffix = 0 or W (most common)
Railroad Retirement Board	
Railroad Retirement/Annuity	Beneficiary Symbol Beneficiary Prefix Claim Number Blank Payee Code
Railroad Unemployment/Sickness	Social Security Number
Social Security Administration	
Social Security	Claim Number
Supplemental Security Income.	Claim Number
Department of Veterans Affairs	
VA Compensation and Pension	Claim Number Payee Code
Department of Labor	
Miners Benefit/Black Lung	Type of Payment

E. Identifying Non-Treasury Disbursed Payments

Identifying the Paying Agency/Payment Type for Non-Treasury Disbursed Payments

Field 7 "Company Entry Description" (Company/Batch Header Record)

Paying Agency/Payment Type	Field 7 Contents
Air Force	
Active Duty	AF_PAY_J_ _
Active Duty Allotments	AF_MP_ALLT
Annuity	AF_RET_PAY
Retirement	AF_RET_PAY
Retirement Pay Allotments	AF_RP_ALLT
Army	
Active Duty	ARMYACTIVE
Annuity	ARMY_BEN_ _
Reserve	ARMY_RC_ _ _
Retirement	ARMY_RET_ _
Marine Corps	
Active Duty	Mar_Active
Active Duty Allotments	MCACTALLOT
Annuity	MarCorAnn_
Retirement	MarCorRet_
Retirement Pay Allotments	MCRETALLOT
Reserve	MarCorRes_
Navy	
Active Duty	NAVY_ACT_ _
Active Duty Allotments	NAVY_ALT_ _
Annuity	NAVY_ANN_ _
Retirement	NAVY_RET_ _
Retirement Pay Allotments	NAVY_RPA_ _
Reserve Drill Pay	NAVY_RDP_ _

Identifying the Payee for Non-Treasury Disbursed Payments

IF the payment type is . . .	THEN Field 7 contents identify the payee by . . .

Air Force
Active Duty
Active Duty Allotment
Annuity ──────────────────── Individual's SSN
Reserve
Retirement
Retirement Pay Allotment

Army
Active Duty
Annuity ──────────────────── Individual's SSN
Reserve
Retirement

Marine Corps
Active Duty .... Letters "KR"
Active Duty Allotment
Annuity
Retirement ──────────────────── Individual's SSN
Retirement Pay Allotment
Reserve

Navy
Active Duty
Active Duty Allotment
Annuity
Retirement ──────────────────── Individual's SSN
Retirement Pay Allotment
Reserve

F. Garnishment of Federal Benefits

Garnishment is the execution, levy, attachment, or other legal process involving a written instruction issued by a court, a State or State agency, a municipality or municipal corporation or a State child support enforcement agency. This includes a lien arising by operation of law for overdue child support or an order to freeze the assets in an account, to effect a garnishment against a debtor.

Financial institutions are subject to the requirements of Title 31 of the Code of Federal Regulations, Part 212 (31 CFR Part 212) which requires financial institutions to take certain actions upon receipt of garnishment orders.

Appendix A contains guidelines that financial institutions can reference when a garnishment order is received for an account into which Federal benefit payments have been directly deposited. Appendix A can be found at the conclusion of this Chapter or is available at:
http://www.fms.treas.gov/greenbook/guidelines_garnish0311.pdf

Financial institutions that receive a garnishment order are required to determine the sum of protected Federal benefits deposited to the account during a two month period, and ensure that the account holder has access to an amount equal to that sum or to the current balance of the account, whichever is lower."

31 CFR Part 212 applies to the following Federal programs:

- Social Security and Supplemental Security Income benefits administered by the Social Security Administration;

- Veterans benefits administered by the Department of Veterans Affairs;

- Federal Railroad retirement unemployment and sickness benefits administered by the Railroad Retirement Board; and

- Civil Service Retirement System and Federal Employee Retirement System benefits administered by the Office of Personnel Management.

To assist financial institutions, Treasury/FMS is encoding an "XX" in Positions 54-55 of the "Company Entry Description" Field of the Batch Header Record for ACH/PPD and ACH/CCD payments that are designated as Federal benefit payments that are exempt from garnishment. This encoding allows financial institutions to determine whether a Federal direct deposit payment is an exempt Federal benefit payment. **Financial institutions may rely on the presence of an "XX" encoded in Positions 54-55 of the "Company Entry Description" Field to identify a Federal benefit payment exempt from garnishment.**

See examples next page.

EXAMPLES:

Benefit Payment Type	Company Entry Description (Positions 54-63) – Prior to the Garnishment Rule	Company Entry Description Garnishment Rule (Positions 54-63) – With the Garnishment Rule
Social Security	SOC SEC	XXSOC SEC
Supplemental Security Income	SUPP SEC	XXSUPP SEC
Railroad Retirement	RR RET	XXRR RET

Because it is possible that a commercial payment could also have an "XX" encoded in Positions 54-55, financial institutions must verify that the payment is a Federal payment. This can be confirmed either by searching for a "2" in the "Originator Status Code" Field in the Batch Header Record (Position 79) OR by reviewing the description of the payment in the ACH Batch Header Record Company Entry Description to ensure that the payment is one of the exempt Federal Benefit Types shown in Appendix X on the GreenBook main page.

Appendix

The publication "Guidelines for Garnishments of Accounts Containing Federal Benefit Payments" has been included in this chapter as an appendix starting on the next page.

3 Nonreceipt

Overview

This chapter describes the role(s) of the Financial Institution in resolving a claim of non-receipt for a Federal payment.

In this Chapter...

A: General Information on Nonreceipt Claims

NACHA Operating Rules require consumer payments (including Federal salary, travel payments, and benefit payments) be made available for withdrawal by the recipient no later than the opening of business on the settlement date (provided the entries are made available to the Receiving Depository Financial Institution (RDFI) by its ACH operator no later than 5 p.m. on the banking day prior to the settlement date). It is imperative that RDFIs review procedures for posting payments and funds availability to ensure compliance with 31 CFR Part 210 and NACHA Operating Rules. Any RDFI can be held liable for ACH payments not processed timely or correctly. If the Federal government sustains a loss as a result of the financial institution's improper handling of an entry, the financial institution is liable to the Federal government for the loss, up to the amount of the entry.

It is extremely important that all RDFI personnel, especially branch, teller, and customer service representatives are properly trained to locate payments, specifically those which are "memo posted" or post prior to the settlement date. Close to 75 percent of "missing" Federal payments are at the RDFI when the recipient calls to inquire. Thorough research will limit misinformation and subsequent unnecessary nonreceipt claims and simultaneously increase confidence in Direct Deposit as a payment method.

If it is ultimately determined that the RDFI did not receive a payment, the benefit recipient may contact the issuing agency to open a claim of nonreceipt. The issuing agency in turn notifies the Department of the Treasury, Financial Management Service (FMS). FMS will initiate contact with the RDFI in an attempt to locate or resolve a claim of non-receipt.

RDFI role in response to customer inquiry on the status of a Direct Deposit Federal Payment

RDFIs should be aware of the following situations that often result in unnecessary nonreceipt claims. The RDFI should make every reasonable attempt to locate a payment prior to redirecting a recipient to the authorizing Federal agency. RDFI employees should have an understanding of the various posting techniques utilized to assist customers who are concerned with the status of their direct deposit.

Determine if the payment was posted late

- RDFI should be able to explain why there was a delay

Determine if the payment was memo posted

- RDFI customer service personnel may sometimes be unaware of, or do not check for "memo posted" items. "Memo-posting" is a temporary credit applied to a payee's account during the day. Memo-posted transactions are finalized in the RDFIs end of day processing.

Determine if the payment was posted early

- Due to volume and processing considerations the RDFI may receive ACH payment files a few days prior to their settlement dates. "Early posting" occurs when an RDFI posts a payment to a recipient's account prior to the settlement date.

Determine if a third party processor is used and confirm funds availability through the processor

- RDFI should confirm if the funds were made available to the recipient.

Determine if the payment was an exception item

- The RDFI should be aware that a payment may have been posted incorrectly, manually posted, or returned due to incorrect account information.

-
In some instances the RDFI may never receive a payment for the recipient. Ask the recipient if he/she has:

- Changed Financial Institutions
- Revoked the Direct Deposit authorization
- Verified entitlement with the authorizing Federal agency

Note: The RDFI should process an NOC entry if they are responsible for the change information. The RDFI may request the benefit recipient to update their information with the issuing agency if the customer has a closed account, new account, etc.

Title 31 CFR 210.8(b)(2) specifically addresses the liability placed on RDFIs for the correct preparation of ENRs and NOCs.

B: Initiating a formal claim of Nonreceipt

If all efforts to locate the payment(s) have failed, the RDFI should instruct the recipient to file a nonreceipt claim directly with the authorizing Federal agency. .The table below lists Federal agencies by types of payments.

Type of Payment	Action
Federal Salary and allotments (including military and civilian pay) Military Active Duty allotments	Advise recipient to contact his/her payroll office. *Note: Coast Guard Active Duty and Allotments (785) 339-3506.*
Military Retirement/Annuity/Allotments	Advise recipient to contact the appropriate military branch. Refer to Contacts, Chapter 7.
Travel Payments	Advise recipient to contact his/her finance/ travel office

Type of Payment	Action
TreasuryDirect	Refer to Contacts, Chapter 7.
Vendor, Miscellaneous, and All Other Payment Types	Advise recipient to contact the Federal Agency that authorized the payment. Refer to Contacts, Chapter 7..

C: Nonreceipt Process

Upon notification from the recipient that a payment has not been received, the authorizing Federal agency will notify the Financial Management Service (FMS). FMS will research the claim either via the Tele-TRACE process or traditional FMS form 150.2 and 150.1 to determine the status of the claim.

Legal References Supporting Treasury Non-Receipt Investigation

1. 12 USC 3413(k)(2): Disclosure Necessary for Proper Administration of Programs of Certain Government Authorities

12 USC 3413 (k)(2) of the Right to Financial Privacy Act provides: "Nothing in this title shall apply to the disclosure by the financial institution of information contained in the financial records of any customer to any Government authority that certifies, disburses, or collects payments, where the disclosure of such information is necessary to and such information is used solely for the purpose of ... the investigation or recovery of an improper Federal payment..."

2. 31 CFR Part 210.3(c): Federal Government Participation in the Automated Clearing House (ACH)

Specifically, 31 CFR Part 210.3(c) provides: "Any person or entity that originates or receives a Government entry agrees to be bound by this part and to comply with all instructions and procedures issued by the Service under this part including the Treasury Financial Manual and the Green Book." The Green Book can be downloaded at the Financial Management Service's website at http://www.fms.treas.gov/greenbook.

3. Green Book, Chapter 4 Returns

The Green Book Section on Returns states that: "Un-postable payments must be returned so that they are received by the Government Disbursing Office (ODFI) no later than the opening of business on the second banking day following the settlement date of the original entry. Under no circumstances should a financial institution hold payments indefinitely in a suspense account, or by any other means, no should payments otherwise be held if any of the conditions apply on when to return a payment. Holding payments may constitute a breach of the financial institution's warranty for the handling of federal government ACH payments under regulations codified in 31 CFR Part 210."

Tele-TRACE Nonreceipt Claims Process

FMS has partnered with several Federal agencies to research Direct Deposit nonreceipt claims via telephone (Tele-TRACE). FMS representatives from the Philadelphia Financial Center (PFC) will call the RDFI directly to resolve claims of nonreceipt. FMS has access to all of the payment information and will seek assistance in identifying a checklist of items:

1. Verification of payment status (posted, funds held, returned, etc)

> Question: Did the item in question post to the account number provided on the date of payment?

2. Verification that the intended payee received the payment

> Question: Does the payee's name appear on the account?

3. Situations where the recipient's name is not on the account (If it is determined that an item has posted to an improper account FMS will make a request for the return of those funds subject to availability)

> Question: Can you provide the date the funds were returned and the reason code used? Do you require an R06 (Returned per ODFI Request) letter from Treasury to return these funds?

4. Situations where the recipient did not receive the payment on settlement date

> Question: Were the funds posted early or late, can the RDFI provide a reasonable explanation as to why?

5. Payments posted manually, due to account closure or invalid account information

> RDFIs should originate a Notification of Change (NOC) entry if corrections are needed for future payments. See Chapter 6, Notification of Change and the NACHA Operating Rules for detailed instructions.

Note: FMS may also request the name, mailing address and telephone number of the improper recipient under the authority of 12 USC 3413(k) (Right to Financial Privacy Act of 1978).

When the reason for nonreceipt has been determined, FMS will mail the recipient a letter information him/her of the resolution.

Keep in mind that RDFIs can be help liable for ACH payments not processed timely or correctly. If the Federal government sustains a loss as a result of a financial institution's improper handling of an entry, the financial institution is liable to the Federal government for the loss, up to the amount of the entry.

Payment Trace Requests: Manual Nonreceipt Claims Process
FMS 150.2

This is a sample of form FMS 150.2

OMB No. 1510-0045

DATE	TRACE REQUEST	DIRECT DEPOSIT

TRACE NUMBER	ROUTING NUMBER	CUSTOMER'S NAME	AMOUNT
		CUSTOMER'S CLAIM NUMBER	PAYMENT DATE
		DEPOSITOR ACCOUNT NUMBER	TYPE OF ACCOUNT
		TYPE OF PAYMENT / DISCRETIONARY DATA	

FMS FORM 150.2

For Paperwork Reduction Act Statement
and Burden Estimate Statement See
Reverse Side "Financial Organization Copy"

The FMS 150.2 is used to trace payments dated the current month or previous month. Upon receipt of the FMS 150.2, the RDFI should follow these steps:

1. Verify the status of the payment in question by making all attempts to locate the payment at the RDFI.

2. Credit the payment immediately if the payment was not previously credited or returned.

3. Return the payment by ACH if it cannot be credited for any reason.

4. Use the recipient's copy of the FMS 150.2 to notify the recipient of the disposition of the payment.

5. Originate an NOC entry if corrections are needed for future payments. See Chapter 6, Notification of Change and the NACHA Operating Rules for detailed instructions.

6. The RDFI should inform the recipient of the payment status.

This is a sample of form FMS 150.1

DEPARTMENT OF THE TREASURY
FINANCIAL MANAGEMENT SERVICE
REGIONAL FINANCIAL CENTER

DIRECT DEPOSIT COORDINATOR

DATE OF REQUEST
_____

❑ SECOND REQUEST

DATE OF ORIGINAL REQUEST
_____

Dear Financial Organization Representative:

One of your customers has filed a claim for nonreceipt stating that their direct deposit payment has not been credited to their account. Your customer authorized the payment indicated below to be sent to your financial organization through Treasury's Direct Deposit Program.

TRACE NO.
_____

RECEIVING FINANCIAL ORGANIZATION ROUTING NO.
_____

INDIVIDUAL *(Customer's Name)*
_____

DEPOSITOR'S ACCOUNT NO.   TYPE OF ACCOUNT
_____

PREFIX INDIVIDUAL ID *(Customer's Claim No.)* SUFFIX
_____

PAYMENT DATE
_____

TYPE OF PAYMENT
_____

AMOUNT
_____

DISCRETIONARY CODE
_____

Treasury's records show that the payment was authorized and sent to your financial organization through the Federal Reserve Banking System.

Please research your records, mark the block in the Financial Organization Action Section below that describes the action taken by your financial organization, sign the Financial Center Copy and return **within 3 days to:**

Department of the Treasury
Financial Management Service
Regional Financial Center
P.O. Box _____
_____

_____
Director, Regional Financial Center

FINANCIAL ORGANIZATION ACTION

❒ The payment described above was credited to the customer's account on (Date) _____

The CUSTOMER'S COPY of this form was completed and forwarded to the customer on (Date) _____

❒ We received the payment listed above. The payment was returned to the Federal Reserve on (Date) _____

❒ We have the payment listed above but cannot post it. We are returning the payment to the Federal Reserve on (Date) _____

❒ Account Owner's name(s) does not match the above stated individual. Action being taken *(Check box below)*:
  ❒ Returning the funds through ACH per Reason Code R06
  ❒ Returning the funds by an Official Bank Check
  ❒ Funds are not available for Return

  Note: *In the Additional Remarks section, please provide the account holder information for the customer who received the payment. (This information is being requested, and may be disclosed, under the authority of 12 USC 3413 (k) - Disclosure Necessary for Proper Administration of Programs of Certain Government Authorities)*

ADDITIONAL REMARKS _____
_____

SIGNATURE
_____

TITLE
_____

DATE
_____

FMS ^FORM 9-09 150.1   FINANCIAL CENTER COPY

The FMS 150.1 is used to trace payments with an issue date two (2) months or older, or as a follow-up notice for previous trace requests, issued on an FMS form 150.2. Upon receipt of an FMS 150.1, the RDFI should follow these steps:

1. Verify the status of the payment in question, by making all attempts to locate the payment at the RDFI.

2. Credit the payment immediately if the payment was not previously credited or returned.

3. Return the payment by ACH if it cannot be credited for any reason.

4. Complete the **FINANCIAL INSTITUTION ACTION** section within three (3) business days of receipt of the form by the RDFI.

5. Return the **DISBURSING OFFICE COPY** to the Government Disbursing Office identified on the form.

6. Use the recipient's copy to notify the recipient of the disposition of the payment.

The RDFI must respond to FMS within three business days by completing and returning the FMS 150.1 to the FMS Regional Financial Center indicated on the form. FMS will verify acceptance of the return.

- If no reply is received, FMS will contact the FI and will pursue the case until it is resolved. If still no reply a letter will be sent to the President of the RDFI.

- The authorizing Federal agency may also contact the RDFI to resolve payment problems.

Keep in mind that the RDFIs can be held liable for ACH payments not processed timely or correctly. If the Federal government sustains a loss as a result of a financial institution's improper handling of an entry, the financial institution is liable to the Federal government for the loss, up to the amount of the entry.

4 Returns

Overview

This chapter describes the return process for Federal payments

In this Chapter...

A: General Information on Returns

All ACH Payments must be returned in accordance with NACHA Operating Rules. An ACH payment must be returned if:

- An enrollment has been terminated and a new enrollment for the same recipient has not been completed.
- The financial institution has actual or constructive knowledge of the death or legal incapacity of a recipient, including a representative payee.
- The financial institution is honoring a Death Notification Entry (DNE) or other notification of death from a Federal agency.
- The account has been closed by the recipient, or the financial institution has closed the account after giving the recipient 30 days written notice (except where fraud is suspected; then the account may be closed immediately).
- There is no current account for the recipient.
- For any other reason the financial institution is unable to credit the payment to the account.

Return Reason Codes (ACH Credits)

The government is able to accept all NACHA-approved return reason codes. Following is a list of some of the more common return reason codes that RDFIs use to return Government credits:

R02　Account Closed

R03　No Account/Unable to Locate Account

R04　Invalid Account Number

R06　Returned per ODFI's Request

R14　Representative Payee Deceased or Unable to Continue in that Capacity

R15　Beneficiary or Account Holder (Other Than a Representative Payee) Deceased

R16　Account Frozen

R17　File Record Edit Criteria (Specify)

RDFIs that learn of the death of a recipient from a source other than the agency are encouraged to use reason code R15 (Beneficiary or Account Holder Deceased) or R14 (Representative Payee Deceased) to notify government agencies of the death. By using these return codes, the RDFI will satisfy both the requirement to return post-death payments and the requirement to notify the agency of the death of the recipient.

If you must return a Federal payment for any reason not listed (i.e., credit sent to a non-transaction account), use reason code "R03" on the return.

Death Notification Entry

The Death Notification Entry (DNE) allows Federal agencies to notify financial institutions of a benefit recipient's death. Only an agency of the Federal Government may originate a DNE. Currently, SSA, OPM, and RRB originate DNEs. Other Federal benefit agencies may originate DNEs at a future date. The DNE is a zero dollar entry with an addenda record. The addenda record contains the date of death, the deceased individual's Social Security Number (SSN), and the amount of the next scheduled benefit payment. Upon receipt of a DNE, the financial institution is encouraged to "flag" the deceased recipient's account to prevent accepting further post-death Federal benefit payments.

Problems Resulting from Incomplete/Improper "Flagging"

Example 1: Joint Accounts

A husband and wife own a joint account. The husband dies. A DNE is sent from the Federal benefit agency to the RDFI. The RDFI receives the DNE and the account is "flagged". The wife becomes eligible for widow's benefits, and a benefit payment is sent to the joint account. Since the account is "flagged," the RDFI improperly returns the widow's benefits with a reason code of R15 (beneficiary or account holder deceased). The agency receives the returned benefit and processes an improper death termination for the widow. The agency also sends an improper DNE for the widow to the RDFI.

Solution: To protect joint account holders, the account should be "flagged" with another piece of identifying information (i.e., deceased name, SSN). This allows the joint account holder to continue receiving his/her own payments. If this is not possible, a new account with a new Direct Deposit authorization should be established.

Example 2: Erroneous DNE

A recipient is receiving benefits. An improper report of death is received by the Federal benefit agency for the recipient. A DNE is sent from the agency to the RDFI and the account is "flagged". The recipient discovers the problem and presents proof to the agency and the RDFI of the error in the fact of death. The agency resends the benefit payment to the recipient's account, which is still "flagged". The RDFI improperly returns benefits with a reason code for death of R15 (beneficiary or account holder deceased) to the agency. The agency receives the returned benefit and re-processes the death termination. The agency sends an improper DNE once again to the RDFI.

Solution: Always remember to remove any "flags" on an account when a report of death proves to be erroneous.

Effect of Returning a Payment

Any returned payment automatically revokes the Direct Deposit authorization and may stop further payments from the Federal agency to a recipient's account. The recipient should contact the authorizing Federal agency to resume payments.

Notice of Misdirected Payment

In accordance with Code 31 CFR Part 210. If an RDFI becomes aware that an agency has originated an ACH credit entry to an account that is not owned by the payee whose name appears in the ACH payment information, the RDFI shall promptly notify the agency. An RDFI that originates a Notification of Change (NOC) entry with the correct account and/or Routing and Transit Number information, or returns the original ACH credit entry to the agency with the appropriate return reason code, shall be deemed to have satisfied this requirement.

Manual Posting of Payments

Financial Institutions may conduct a manual search of their unpostable ACH payments to determine i the payment can be posted.

RDFIs may be held liable for ACH payments not processed timely or correctly. If the Federal government sustains a loss as a result of a financial institution's improper handling of an entry, the financial institution is liable to the Federal government for the loss, up to the amount of the entry.

Holding Payments in Suspense Accounts

Under no circumstances should a financial institution hold payments indefinitely in a suspense account, or by any other means, nor should payments otherwise be held if any of the conditions apply on when to return a payment. Holding payments may constitute a breach of the financial institution's warranty for the handling of Federal government ACH payments under regulations codified in 31 CFR Part 210.

Recipients Without Current Accounts

A financial institution should not open a new account in response to an unpostable payment. If a recipient's account has been closed, the financial institution must return any subsequent payments made by the Federal agency to the account. If the recipient closes the account and opens a new account the recipient must establish a new Direct Deposit authorization.

B: Returning Payments Through the ACH

ACH Correct Preparation of Returns

It is essential that RDFI employees preparing returns have access to data in the original item originated by the Government Disbursing Office. If a processor is used, RDFIs should be sure that the return entry is properly formatted to include the data from the original entry.

"When an Automated Return Entry is prepared, the original Company/Batch Header Record, the original Entry Detail Record, and the Company/Batch Control Record are copied for return to the Originator." (NACHA Operating Rules) If accurate data is not provided in the return entry, the Government Disbursing Office will dishonor the return.

The following four fields must be identical to the original payment data:

1. Trace number (provided in the entry detail record)

2. Effective entry date

3. Amount of payment

4. Individual ID number (i.e., claim number. See Table below)

Note: *Financial institutions using data processors could received reformatted data which may contain errors or omissions.* **The original payment information must be used in its exact format to avoid rejections.**

Financial institutions should carefully track returned benefit payments to ensure that the returns are not dishonored. This could create an additional liability for the financial institution in a reclamation case.

Claim Number Structure Table

The following table represents correct claim number structures used in formatting returns.

Agency	Claim Number Structure	Example
Social Security Administration	999999999XX 999999999X 999999999	123456789C1 123456789A 123456789
Office of Personnel Management	Xb9999999bXb Xb9999999b9b	F_1234567_W_ A_1234567_0_
Department of Veterans Affairs	999999999b99b99 99999999b99b99	162306890_10_01 12345678_00_06
Railroad Retirement Board		
Retirement/Annuity	XXX999999999b9b Xbb999999bbbb9b XXbZZZZZ9bbbb9b	WCA123456789_7_ A__123456____1_ WD_000006____8_
Unemployment/Sickness	bbb999999999	___123456789
Department of Labor	999999999XXbXXb	123456789LW_MB_

Key: X = alphanumeric, 9 = numeric, b = blank, Z = zero filled, _ = space

C: Returning Partial Payments in Response to Notices of Reclamation

If a partial payment is being returned in response to a Notice of Reclamation, it must be returned by check. *In no other case should ACH returns by made by check.* Please refer to Chapter 5, Reclamations, for more information.

Note: If the original payment data has been discarded, a financial institution may be forced to return an ACH payment by check. The financial institution will receive credit. However, in these cases, credit will be delayed due to manual processing. Note that under NACHA Operating Rules, records of all entries including return and adjustment entries must be retained for six years from the date the entry was transmitted.

The table below shows how to return a partial payment by check in response to a Notice of Reclamation.

Step	Action
1	Send the Government Disbursing Office a check payable as indicated on item C-3b on the Notice of Reclamation. DO NOT SEND THE CHECK TO THE ORIGINATING FEDERAL AGENCY.
2	• Attach a cover letter listing the following information for each payment subject to return: • effective entry date • amount of payment • individual ID number (i.e., SSN/claim number) • reason for return If not available, provide the following information: • recipient's name • recipient's SSN or other applicable Federal Government ID number • date of death • name of originating Federal agency The cover letter must always include: • recipient's name • name of originating Federal agency **Provide the name, address, and telephone number of the financial institution contact.**

D: Dishonored Returns

ACH return items will be dishonored by the Government Disbursing Office if discrepancies exist between the data on the return item and the data on the original payment.

Most Common Errors

For Treasury-disbursed payments, four fields are read on return items. If any one of these four fields is not identical to the original payment data, Treasury's system will dishonor the return.

1. Trace number (provided in the addenda record)

2. effective entry date (i.e., payment date)

3. amount of payment

4. individual ID number (i.e., claim number)

The discretionary data field on the return item should be left blank ONLY if it was blank in the original ACH entry. Some financial institutions may have to make an additional "dump run" for the discretionary data. If the field contains data in the original entry, the data must be included in the return entry.

Note that a VA claim number may be an 8-digit number with a blank in the leading space of the individual ID field. If the space is ignored, and the number is left-justified, the return will be dishonored. (See the claim number structure table on page 4-5.)

If a financial institution receives a dishonored return, the information in the return should be corrected and a new return should be originated in accordance with NACHA Operating Rules.

Dishonored Return Codes:

- R61 - Misrouted Return

- R67 - Duplicate Return

- R68 - Untimely Return

- R69 - Field Errors (the error(s) will be identified in the addendum record on the dishonored file positions 59-79. The two-digit code, separated by an asterisk, will be written for each error found.)
    01 - Return Contains Incorrect DFI Account Number
    02 - Return Contains Incorrect Original Entry Trace Number
    03 - Return Contains Incorrect Dollar Amount
    04 - Return Contains Incorrect Individual Identification Number/Identification Number
    05 - Return Contains Incorrect Transaction Code
    06 - Return Contains Incorrect Company Identification Number
    07 - Return Contains an Invalid Effective Entry Date*
        *Effective September 21, 2007

- R70 - Permissible Return Entry Not Accepted

E: Obtaining a Refund due from the Government, including Payments Returned in Error

If you are due a refund from the government under ACH, regardless of whether you have returned too much, or returned the wrong item(s), or the government debited you too much (e.g., on an ACH reclamation), follow these instructions to claim your refund.

 Note: *Any payment returned for "death" will cancel both the Direct Deposit authorization and the recipient's entitlement to that payment.*

Please also note: an RDFI is not required to advance credit to the recipient for a payment returned in error. However, if it did advance credit, the RDFI should state this in any communication with the Federal Government.

Action Steps

1. Contact the Federal Agency that authorized the payment. Do not contact the Government Disbursing Office, e.g., the Treasury Department

Payment Type	Contact
OPM Annuity (formerly Civil Service Retirement) "CIVIL SERV"	U.S. Office of Personnel Management P.O. Box 45 Boyers, PA 16017 (724) 794-2005
Social Security "SOC SEC"	SSA Program Service Center (Refer to p. 4-9 and 4-10 for appropriate addresses).
Supplemental Social Security Income "SUPP SEC"	Social Security Administration Certification and Accounting Branch, Analyst Room 3-A-2 East High Rise Building 6401 Security Boulevard Baltimore, MD 21235 (410) 966-5353
Bureau of the Fiscal Service *"TreasuryDirect"*	Bureau of the Fiscal Service Customer Assistance Branch P.O. Box 426 Parkersburg, WV 26102-0426 (304) 480-7591 *Note:* Include with your letter a debit advice, Return Item-Credit Form, and any other documents that confirm the duplicate or erroneous return.
VA Compensation or Pension "VA BENEFIT"	None. *Note:* Returned VA payments cannot be recalled. They will be reissued to the recipient's home address.
Railroad Retirement Board	Railroad Retirement Board Direct Deposit Coordinator (312) 751-4704
For all other payment types	The Federal agency's local office listed in the telephone directory.

2. Promptly notify the recipient of the error.

If you erroneously reported death on the ACH return, advise the recipient to contact the originating Federal agency immediately to reactivate payments.

Advise the recipient that the returned payment may be sent via check to his/her home. The recipient should contact the Federal agency to ensure his/her current home address is on record and that payments are handled properly.

3. Be aware that your incorrect notification of death to a Federal authorizing agency (OPM, SSA, RRB), may result in a DNE being sent by the agency.

If a DNE is received, be sure to remove any electronic indicator or flag that would automatically return future payments to the account.

4. Initiate a new enrollment to reactivate ACH payments. Please see Chapter 1, Enrollments, for more information.

Note: *The financial institution's copy of the original enrollment form may be photocopied and sent to the Federal agency if all the information is still correct.*

Additional Information on *TreasuryDirect* Payments made in Error/Duplicate

If a payment is made in error, or if a duplicate payment is made, the financial institution will receive either a written or electronic notice from TreasuryDirect that will include the following:

- deposit account name
- deposit account number
- date of the improper payment
- amount of the improper payment

SSA Program Service Centers

Note: *All SSA cycled payments (dated the 2nd, 3rd, and 4th Wednesday of the month), regardless of the Social Security number, are disbursed by the Philadelphia Treasury RFC.*

SSA Program Service Center	SSN Range	Treasury RFC
Social Security Administration Northeastern Program Service Center 1 Jamaica Center Jamaica, NY 11432-3830	001-134	Philadelphia
Social Security Administration Mid-Atlantic Program Service Center 300 Spring Garden Street Philadelphia, PA 19123	135-222 232-236 577-584 596-599 691-699	Philadelphia

SSA Program Service Center	SSN Range	Treasury RFC
Social Security Administration Southwestern Program Service Center 2001 Twelfth Ave., North Birmingham, AL 35285	223-231 237-267 400-428 587-595 654-658 667-675 681-690 752-763	Philadelphia
Social Security Administration Great Lakes Program Service Center 600 West Madison Street Chicago, IL 60661	268-302 316-399 700-799	Kansas City
Social Security Administration Mid-America Program Service Center 601 East 12th Street Kansas City, MO 64106	303-315 429-500 505-515 528-585 627-645 648-649 659-665 676-679	Kansas City
Social Security Administration Western Program Service Center P.O. Box 2000 Richmond, CA 94802	501-504 516-524 526-576 586 600-626	San Francisco

What to do if there are Duplicate Returns

The table below shows what to do if there are duplicate returns.

IF . . .	THEN . . .	AND . . .
two identical ACH returns are made for the same payment	the Government Disbursing Office will automatically return the duplicate return	no further action is required by the financial institution.
an ACH return was sent and the same payment was returned by check the financial institution has been debited (TFS, Notice of Debit) for a payment that was already returned	the financial institution should promptly write a letter of explanation to the Federal agency that authorized the payment and include copies of the following: • financial institution's claim for a refund • debit advice • other documentation that confirms the duplicate return/debit action	the financial institution awaits further notification from the authorizing Federal agency. *Note: Only the Federal agency that authorized the payment can make a refund.*

Restoring Funds

The authorizing Federal agency will restore the funds after researching and verifying the request. The restoration will be made, via the appropriate method, as mutually agreed by the Federal agency, the financial institution, and the recipient.

5 Reclamations

Overview

Section 1 defines reclamation and provides some background information on the subject. Section 2 covers an RDFI's liability in the reclamation process. Topics include full and limited liability, calculating the limited liability amount, and exceptions to the liability rule. Section 3 gives RDFIs guidance on processing reclamations and provides an updated contact list for individuals needing additional information/assistance with reclamations.

Section 1: Background

Reclamation is a procedure used by the Federal government (government) to recover benefit payments made through the Automated Clearing House (ACH) to the account of a recipient who died or became legally incapacitated or a beneficiary who died before the date of the payment(s).

The government's right to reclaim funds is established in Title 31 of the Code of Federal Regulations Part 210, Subpart B, and Section 210.10(a). The government's reclamation process is found in 31 CFR 210.9 through 210.14. The reclamation provisions of 31 CFR 210 completely preempt the reclamation provisions of the NACHA Operating Rules with respect to Federal benefit payments.

By accepting a recurring benefit payment from the government, a receiving depository financial institution (RDFI) agrees to the provisions of 31 CFR 210, including the reclamation and debiting of the RDFI's Federal Reserve Bank account for any reclamation for which it is liable. This liability provision of the Federal reclamation regulations is part of the contract between the government and the RDFI. The two parties thereby agree to share liability for post-death payments. This contract is renewed by the RDFI each time it accepts and credits an ACH payment on behalf of a depositor.

Note: In this chapter, "death" always means the death or legal incapacity of a recipient or the death of a beneficiary. And "government" always means the Federal government.

Payments Subject to Reclamation

Only government benefit payments are subject to reclamation.

Payments Subject to Reclamations	Payments not Subject to Reclamations
Social Security benefit or disability (SSA)	Federal salary, allotments, and travel payments
Supplemental Security Income (SSI)	U.S. savings bond payments
Black Lung disability (Dept. of Labor)	Vendor/miscellaneous payments
Military and Coast Guard retirement, including allotments from military retired pay (DFAS)	IRS tax refunds
	Discretionary allotments
Civil Service annuity (OPM)	Public Debt payments (TreasuryDirect)
Veterans Administration benefits (VA)	Other types of Federal ACH payments
Railroad Retirement Board (RRB) annuity	
US Coast Guard	
Worker's compensation (FECA)	*Note: For post-death payments not affected by reclamation, adjustments are made only between the authorizing Federal agency and the recipient's survivors or estate*
DC Pensions	
Compensation Act (Dept. of Labor)	
Any other Federal retirement or annuity	

Section 2: Liability of a Receiving Depository Financial Institution (RDFI)

A. Full Liability

An RDFI is liable for ALL benefit payments received after the death or legal incapacity of a recipient or death of a beneficiary; unless the RDFI meets the qualifications for limiting its liability (see B. Limiting Liability below).

If the RDFI fails to meet the qualifications for limiting its liability, the RDFI will be held liable for all post-death payments received after the death or legal incapacity of a recipient or death of a beneficiary. The RDFI will be debited for the full amount of the reclamation; this debit action will be final.

Note: *If no post-death payment has been received at the time the RDFI learns of the death, the RDFI may also contact the paying agency (see Contacts, Chapter 8).*

B. Limiting Liability

An RDFI may qualify to limit its liability if it:

- certifies it did not have actual or constructive knowledge* of the recipient's death or incapacity at the time of the deposit of any post-death benefit payments;

- returns all post-death benefit payments it receives after it learns of the death; and

- responds to the Notice of Reclamation (FMS-133), completely and adequately, so that it is received by the Government Disbursing Office within 60 days from the date of the notice.

*Note: In this chapter "constructive knowledge" of the death means that the RDFI would have learned of the death if it had followed commercially reasonable business practices.

Exception to Liability Rule

An RDFI is not liable for post-death benefit payments sent to a recipient acting as a representative payee or fiduciary on behalf of a beneficiary, if the beneficiary was deceased at the time the authorization (Direct Deposit enrollment) was executed and the RDFI did not have actual or constructive knowledge of the death of the beneficiary.

C. Calculating the Limited Liability Amount

If an RDFI qualifies for **limited liability**, the RDFI will only be debited for the **45-day amount**.

The **45-day amount** is the dollar amount of the post-death benefit payments received within 45 calendar days following the death.

 Note: The limited liability amount may not exceed the outstanding total on the Notice of Reclamation. The outstanding total is the total amount of all the post-death payments.

Table 2-A Calculating the Limited Liability Amount

Example 1: Four payments of $200 each were received after death. *The first payment was received within 45 days after the date of death (i.e., 45-day amount = $200). The RDFI had no actual or constructive knowledge at the time the post-death payments were received or withdrawn.[1] No additional payments were received after the RDFI had knowledge.[2]*

	Ex.1	Ex.2	Ex.3	Ex.4	Ex.5
Total Amount of post-death payments on the Notice of Reclamation	$ 800	$ 800	$ 800	$ 800	$ 800
Amount of the Account Balance paid by RDFI in response to the Notice of Reclamation 3	$ 300	$ 300	$ 750	$ 0	$ 800
Amount due from withdrawers	$ 500	$ 500	$ 50	$ 800	$ 0
Amount collected by government from withdrawers	$ 250	$ 500	$ 0	$ 0	$ 0
Outstanding total	$ 250	$ 0	$ 50	$ 800	$ 0
Amount to be debited from the RDFI's Federal Reserve account = (lesser of Outstanding Total or 45-day amount)	$ 200	$ 0	$ 50	$ 200	$ 0

[1] RDFI had no actual or constructive knowledge of the death at the time of deposit or withdrawal of any post-death benefit payments.

[2] RDFI returns all post-death benefit payments it receives after it learns of the death.

[3] RDFI accurately responds to the Notice of Reclamation so that the appropriate amount is received by the Government Disbursing Office within 60 days of the date on the Notice.

Example 2: Four payments of $200 each were received after death. *Three of the payments were received before the RDFI had actual or constructive knowledge of the death.[1] The 4th payment was received by the RDFI after it had received a DNE and the RDFI promptly returned the payment using an R15 return reason code.[2] The 1st and 2nd payments were received within 45 days following the date of death (4th payment will not be listed on the Notice of Reclamation since it was promptly returned by the RDFI).*

	Ex. 1	Ex. 2	Ex. 3	Ex. 4	Ex. 5
Total Amount of post-death payments on the Notice of Reclamation	$ 600	$ 600	$ 600	$ 600	$ 600
Amount of the Account Balance paid by RDFI in response to the Notice of Reclamation 3	$ 300	$ 300	$ 550	$ 0	$ 600
Amount due from withdrawers	$ 300	$ 300	$ 50	$ 600	$ 0
Amount collected by government from withdrawers	$ 50	$ 300	$ 0	$ 0	$ 0
Outstanding total	$ 250	$ 0	$ 50	$ 600	$ 0
Amount to be debited from the RDFI's Federal Reserve account = (lesser of Outstanding Total or 45-day amount)	$ 250	$ 0	$ 50	$ 400	$ 0

[1] RDFI had no actual or constructive knowledge of the death at the time of deposit or withdrawal of any post-death benefit payments.

[2] RDFI returns all post-death benefit payments it receives after it learns of the death.

[3] RDFI accurately responds to the Notice of Reclamation so that the appropriate amount is received by the Government Disbursing Office within 60 days of the date on the Notice.

Section 3: Reclamation Procedures

A. Notification of Death

An RDFI must immediately return any post-death benefit payments received after the RDFI becomes aware of the death or legal incapacity of a recipient. If the RDFI learns of the death or legal incapacity of a recipient from a source other than the federal agency, the RDFI must notify the sending agency of the recipient's death. An ACH return using return reason code R15 or R14 constitutes proper notification to the Federal agency. When returning payments the RDFI should ensure that the date of death in the addenda record be in YYMMDD format. The RDFI should also provide notification to the account owners, as a courtesy.

Notification of death by any source constitutes notification for all Federal benefit payments received by the recipient. The following are some examples of ways that the RDFI may learn of the death of their account holders:

- Receipt of a Death Notification Entry (DNE) - A DNE is a notification of a benefit recipients death sent from an originating government agency [e.g., SSA, RRB, or OPM] to the RDFI.

- Receipt of a federal government Notice of Reclamation, (FMS-133).

- Any contact or request to withdraw funds from an Estate, Executor, Administrator, Public Administrator, Personal Representative, Conservator or other representative of such Estate. Note: Any release to an executor or other party clearly acting on behalf of the deceased person or his/her estate will be deemed by the government to have demonstrated the RDFI's knowledge of the death.

- A pertinent reference to or from a Probate Court, a funeral home, or Letters Testamentary. Any oral or written report of death.

- Any death information obtained by the RDFI's inquiry into a dormant account, or through other RDFI internal screening processes.

- Any personal awareness of the death by the RDFI's staff.

- Any notice received in the mail from any source.

Note: If at the time the RDFI first receives information of death, all or part of the post-death benefit payments have already been withdrawn from the account, the government does not authorize the RDFI to try to recover the funds from the withdrawer. If the RDFI does so, it acts under its own authority in terms of its contract with its depositor or under state law.

Applicable Federal Regulation 31 CFR 210

This regulation defines when an RDFI has actual or constructive knowledge of the death:

An RDFI has actual knowledge of the death or legal incapacity of a recipient or the death of a beneficiary when it receives information that the recipient has died and has had a reasonable opportunity to act on such information. An RDFI has constructive knowledge if the institution would have learned of the death if it had followed commercially reasonable business practices. [31 CFR Part 210.2(b)]

> The phrase "commercially reasonable business practices" is a flexible concept since, for example, what is a commercially reasonable practice for a large bank may not be commercially reasonable for a small rural bank, and vice versa.

What to do upon Notification of Death with Payments Already Posted and Subsequent Payments

When an RDFI receives actual or constructive knowledge of the death, it does not have to wait for a Notice of Reclamation. The RDFI can immediately return all subsequent post-death benefit payments to the Government Disbursing Office. The RDFI must also notify the sending agency of the recipient's death. An ACH return using return reason code R15 or R14 constitutes proper notification to the Federal agency.

R15 Beneficiary Deceased

The beneficiary is the person entitled to the benefits. In this case, there is no representative payee or guardian involved.

R14 Representative Payee (or Guardian) Deceased or Incapacitated

The representative payee (or guardian) is the person who receives benefit payments on behalf of the (under aged or incapacitated) beneficiary. E.g., payment is payable to "John Doe, for [another person]"

Any information of the death received by the RDFI or any of its employees, from whatever source, establishes the full legal liability for ALL SUBSEQUENT post-death Federal benefit payments from all agencies, as well as any post-death benefits in the account, which the RDFI then allows to be withdrawn.

Note: Recipients may be receiving multiple benefit payments from the same or different Federal agencies. An RDFI should ensure that they are returning all federal benefit payments subject to Reclamation.

Holding Payments

Under no circumstances should an RDFI hold payments indefinitely in a suspense account, or by any other means, nor should payments otherwise be held if any of the conditions apply on when to return a payment. Holding payments may constitute a breach of the RDFI's warranty for the handling of Federal government ACH payments under 31 CFR 210 and could result in an RDFI's inability to limit its liability.

Repayment by Survivors

If the survivors or other withdrawers state that the withdrawn post-death payments have already been repaid to the Federal agency, the RDFI should obtain a front and back copy of the check(s) and/or a receipt from the federal agency.

If all post-death payments have been repaid by the survivor(s), the RDFI should not receive a Notice of Reclamation. However, if a Notice of Reclamation is received, the RDFI must complete and return the form to the Government Disbursing Office within 60 days, attaching an explanation and proof of payment (i.e. front and back copy of the check(s). The RDFI is not liable for any post-death payments that have already been repaid to the originating agency.

Handling Survivor Requests not to Return Post-death Benefit Payments

The RDFI may be asked by the survivor(s) not to return post-death benefit payments because the survivor is still entitled to all or part of the payment(s). In such cases, the RDFI should still return the payment and advise the survivor(s) to contact the appropriate Federal benefit agency (see Chapter 7, Contacts) to determine whether a final survivor payment is due.

B. Notice of Reclamation

The Notice of Reclamation (FMS-133) initiates the recovery of post-death benefit payments that have not been returned to the government, for which the RDFI may be liable.

The Notice of Reclamation is mailed to the RDFI by the Government Disbursing Office upon instructions from the authorizing Federal agency. The RDFI's address and routing number are derived from the Financial Organization Master File (FOMF) maintained by Treasury. Each RDFI is responsible for updating the Federal Reserve Banks (FRB) ACH Customer Directory (see Chapter 2, page 2-3, FOMF). If the Notice of Reclamation is mailed to an obsolete address, the RDFI may be held liable for failing to notify the FRB of changes to their mailing address.

 Note: If the full amount listed on the reclamation is returned to the Disbursing Office, the RDFI does NOT need to complete and return the FMS-133.

Table 3-A Notice of Reclamation (Form FMS-133)

The Notice of Reclamation advises the RDFI of...

- the date of death or legal incapacity;

- the amount of post-death payment(s) for which the RDFI may be liable;

- the identity of each payment(s) in question, including:

  1. name of the recipient

  2. individual ID or claim #

  3. reclamation ticket #

  4. date of the payment(s)

  5. Federal agency that authorized the payment(s) and the type of payment(s)

  6. payment trace number(s)

  7. type of account (checking/savings) to which the payment(s) was made

  8. depositor account number

  9. amount of the payment(s).

The FMS-133 consists of six parts (RDFI will receive Parts 1 through 5):

Part 1- Program Agency Copy

Part 2- Program Agency File Copy

Part 3- RDFI Copy

Part 4- Disbursing Office Copy

Part 5- Notice to Account Owners Copy

Part 6- Disbursing Office Pending Copy (RDFI does not receive Part 6)

Note: The reclamation ticket number is located in the top right box of the form to the right of the date (see sample FMS-133). It is important the RDFI retain a copy of the reclamation form for a minimum of three years or until the associated case is closed. The RDFI should file the notice using the reclamation ticket number. In the event that a debit is processed, the RDFI will need to locate the Notice of Reclamation using the ticket number provided on the FRB Statement of Account (see How to Identify Debits using the Reclamation Ticket Number).

Notice of Reclamation (FMS-133), FRONT

Sample: Parts 1-4 The following sample is the same for the Program Agency Copy, Program Agency File Copy, RDFI Copy and Disbursing Office Copy.

For Paperwork Reduction Act Statement
and Burden Estimate Statement See Reverse
Side "Notice to Account Owners" Copy

OMB NO.: 1510-0043
Expiration Date: 02/28/2000

DIRECT ▶DEPOSIT
ELECTRONIC FUNDS TRANSFER
FEDERAL RECURRING PAYMENTS

NOTICE OF RECLAMATION

FROM

DATE　　　　Ticket # 123456789

REC P ENT AND/OR BENEF C ARY NAME	CLA M NUMBER	DATE OF DEATH

DATE OF PAYMENT	AGENCY AND /OR TYPE OF PAYMENT	TRACE NUMBER	TYPE OF ACCOUNT	DEPOSITOR ACCOUNT NUMBER	AMOUNT

AMOUNT OF PAYMENTS RECE VED
W TH N 45 DAYS

OUTSTAND NG TOTAL

A　mmediately mail NOT CE TO ACCOUNT OWNERS (last copy of this form) to current address of the account owner. nform the account owner(s) of any actions your financial institution has taken or intends to take. Sign Certification No. 1 on the back of the D SBURS NG OFF CE COPY.

B　Correct any error in the fact of death, date of death and/or outstanding total on the back of the D SBURS NG OFF CE COPY.

C　Take, as appropriate, one of the four steps below

1　If the outstanding total was previously returned to the Government, attach copies of the front and back of the cancelled checks and/or proof that the payment was returned by ACH. Proceed with step D below.

2　If the amount in the account is equal to or exceeds the outstanding total, prepare one ACH return for each full payment, described above. The ACH return method should always be used when returning one or more full payments. Proceed with step D below.

3　If the amount in the account is less than the outstanding total and there is...

　　a.(1)　only one payment listed above, then return the partial payment by check. (See 3b).

　　a.(2)　more than one payment listed above, then prepare ACH return(s) for amount(s) equal to each full payment. Any remaining amount that does not equal a full payment must be returned by check, (See 3b).

　　b.　Prepare a check made payable to _____
　　　　ONLY FOR AMOUNTS LESS THAN ONE FULL PAYMENT.

　　(Note The amount in the account includes any additions to the account balance made after the receipt of this NOT CE.)

　　Provide the names and addresses of the withdrawers on the back of the D SBURS NG OFF CE COPY. f it is a true statement of fact, you must sign Certification No. 2 on the back of the D SBURS NG OFF CE COPY. Proceed with Step D below.

4　If the amount in the account is zero and no funds are available to return to the Government, provide the names and addresses of the withdrawers on the back of the D SBURS NG OFF CE COPY. f it is a true statement of fact, you must sign Certification No. 2 on the back of the D SBURS NG OFF CE COPY. Proceed with Step D below.

D　Unless the outstanding total is returned by ACH within 45 days of the date on this NOT CE, return the PROGRAM AGENCY and D SBURS NG OFF CE COP ES of this form to the disbursing office address shown in the upper right hand corner of the form.

YOUR FINANCIAL INSTITUTION IS LIABLE TO THE GOVERNMENT FOR THE ABOVE PAYMENT(S) AND FOR ALL GOVERNMENT BENEFIT PAYMENTS RECEIVED AFTER THE DEATH OR LEGAL INCAPACITY OF THE RECIPIENT OR THE DEATH OF THE BENEFICIARY AS SET FORTH IN 31 CFR PART 210. YOU MUST TAKE THE APPROPRIATE STEPS OUTLINED IN A THROUGH D ABOVE AND IN THE GREEN BOOK INSTRUCTIONS IN ORDER TO LIMIT YOUR LIABILITY. (See GREEN BOOK RECLAMATIONS CHAPTER for detailed instructions.)

IF YOU DO NOT RESPOND APPROPRIATELY WITHIN 60 DAYS FROM THE DATE OF THIS REQUEST, YOU WILL NOT LIMIT YOUR LIABILITY AND YOUR FEDERAL RESERVE ACCOUNT OR THE ACCOUNT OF YOUR CORRESPONDENT WILL BE DEBITED FOR THE OUTSTANDING TOTAL

ROUT NG NUMBER:
　　　　TO:

TO BE COMPLETED BY PROGRAM AGENCY
$_____　　$_____
Amount Recovered　　　　Amount to Recover

Signature　　　　　　　　Date

DEPARTMENT OF THE TREASURY
FINANCIAL MANAGEMENT SERVICE
PROGRAM MANAGEMENT DIVISION
FMS 133 (2-97)

FINANCIAL ORGANIZATION COPY

Notice of Reclamation (FMS-133), BACK

Sample: Parts 1-4 The following sample is the same for the Program Agency Copy, Program Agency File Copy, RDFI Copy and Disbursing Office Copy.

THIS BLOCK FOR DISBURSING OFFICE USE

A Notice of Reclamation

Total Amount Due _____ Total Amount Refunded _____

To Be Recovered
By Agency _____

The amount of $ _____ was deposited for credit in the account of the _____ on
                                                                                                    DISBURSING OFFICER

Certificate of Deposit No _____ dated _____

DR 4 20 Confirmed Deposits
CR 4 10 Net D O   Transaction   Station Code _____ _____
                                                                                         DISBURSING OFFICER

Trust Fund or Appropriation Symbol _____ _____
                                                                                         DATE

B Further Action
☐ No further action being taken
☐ Request for Debit for $ _____ forwarded to FRB on _____

THIS BLOCK FOR FINANCIAL INSTITUTION USE

f information on the face of this form is WRONG check appropriate box and enter the corrections below

☐ Recipient/beneficiary did not die financial institution will not take further action

☐ Date of death is wrong Date of death from death certificate is _____

☐ Adjusted Outstanding Total (total of payments received after the correct date of death)
   (The Adjusted Outstanding Total is used by the financial institution if it is less than the OUTSTANDING TOTAL shown on the face of the form) $ _____

☐ Adjusted outstanding total is greater than outstanding total on face of this form (See Green Book for detailed instructions)

F LESS THAN THE OUTSTANDING TOTAL IS BEING PAID PROVIDE THE NAMES AND ADDRESSES OF THE PERSONS WHO WITHDREW FROM THIS ACCOUNT _____
_____
_____

(f the names of withdrawers cannot be determined provide names of co owners or persons with access to the account and explain why names of withdrawers cannot be provided)

CERTIFICATION NO 1

This certifies that the Notice to Account Owners form was mailed to the owners of the account at the addresses on the records of this financial institution on _____
f a correction has been made to the fact or date of death this certifies that the date of death entered above is correct and that this financial institution took prudent measures to assure that the person is alive or that the date of death was erroneous

_____
Signed

_____
itle

_____
Date

CERTIFICATION NO 2

n accordance with 31 CFR 210 this certifies that this financial institution received the Notice of Reclamation on _____ and first learned of the death on _____ The financial institution had no knowledge of the death or legal incapacity of the recipient or death of the beneficiary at the time any of the payments listed were credited to or withdrawn from the account An amount equal to the amount remaining in the account including any additions to the account balance since the receipt of this notice has been paid to the Government

_____
Signed

_____
itle

_____
Date

Notice of Reclamation (FMS-133), FRONT

Sample: Part 5 Below is a sample of Part 5, Notice to Account Owners, of the FMS-133.

For Paperwork Reduction Act Statement
and Burden Estimate Statement See Reverse
Side "Notice to Account Owners" Copy

OMB NO.: 1510-0043
Expiration Date: 02/28/2000

DIRECT DEPOSIT

ELECTRONIC FUNDS TRANSFER
FEDERAL RECURRING PAYMENTS

NOTICE OF RECLAMATION

FROM

DATE   Ticket:123456789

RECP ENT AND/OR BENEF C ARY NAME	CLA M NUMBER	DATE OF DEATH

DATE OF PAYMENT	AGENCY AND /OR TYPE OF PAYMENT	TRACE NUMBER	TYPE OF ACCOUNT	DEPOS TOR ACCOUNT NUMBER	AMOUNT

AMOUNT OF PAYMENTS RECE VED W TH N 45 DAYS	OUTSTAND NG TOTAL

NOTICE TO ACCOUNT OWNERS FROM THE GOVERNMENT

The Government has received information that the person named on this notice is deceased The purpose of this notice is to inform you that by law entitlement to Government benefits for this person ended at death Therefore the Government must recover all payments made after the date of death f there has been an error and this person is not deceased or if the date of death is wrong this notice explains how to correct the mistake f you do not understand this notice please get help from either your financial institution or the Government agency that was making payments

PAYMENTS TO THIS PERSON HAVE BEEN STOPPED

Your financial institution has been asked to return the payments shown on this notice to the Government because they were issued in error The Government has asked your financial institution to send this notice to you the account owner Your financial institution must notify you if it has taken action to recover these funds from the account Contact your financial institution immediately if you do not understand its actions f the Government is unable to collect from the financial institution the full amount of the payments made after death you may be contacted by the agency which made the payments

IF THE PERSON IS NOT DECEASED

f the person is not deceased immediately contact both your financial institution and the agency that made the payments to correct the error The Government regrets any inconvenience this error may cause Your financial institu tion can correct the collection action if it is given satisfactory proof that the person is alive NOTE YOU MUST CONTACT THE AGENCY THAT MADE THE PAYMENTS BECAUSE TH S ERROR HAS STOPPED FURTHER PAYMENTS ONLY THE AGENCY CAN RESTART THE PAYMENTS

NOTICE TO ACCOUNT OWNERS

Notice of Reclamation (FMS-133), BACK

Sample: Part 5 Below is a sample of Part 5, Notice to Account Owners, of the FMS-133.

IF THE DATE OF DEATH IS WRONG

f the date of death shown is wrong immediately show your financial institution a copy of the death certificate which will permit it to make any needed adjustment to the amount it must return to the Government f it is inconvenient to go to the financial institution bring this notice and a death certificate to the agency that made the payments so correction may be made The agency that made the payments is shown using these abbreviations

> SOCIAL SECURITY ADMINISTRATION: RSI-SSA; DIB-SSA; RSI-SSI
> DEPARTMENT OF VETERANS AFFAIRS: VA
> OFFICE OF PERSONNEL MANAGEMENT: OPM
> RAILROAD RETIREMENT BOARD: RRB
> OTHER AGENCY ABBREVIATIONS: AF RET PAY; ARMY RET; ARMY BEN;
> MarCorRet; MarCorAnn; NAVYRET; NAVY ANN; CIADSANNU

SURVIVOR BENEFITS

Persons related to the deceased may qualify for survivor payments Survivors should contact the agency that made payments to determine whether they are eligible

---

NOTICE FOR FINANCIAL INSTITUTION ONLY

Paperwork Reduction Act and Privacy Act Statement

By author ty of 5 USC 301, 12 USC 391, and T t e 31, Code of Federa Regu at ons, Part 210, the nformat on requested on these forms s mandatory n order for Treasury to recover from your organ zat on one or more E ectron c Funds Transfer payments wh ch the rec p ent or benefic ary named was not ent t ed to rece ve. Fa ure to prov de a the requ red nformat on and to return an amount equa to the amount n the account (up to the tota be ng rec a med) before the dead ne may cause Treasury to contact your Federa Reserve bank to automat ca y deb t your account (or that of your correspondent).

Burden Estimate Statement

The est mated average t me (burden hours) assoc ated w th fi ng out th s paper-work s 12 m nutes per respondent or recordkeeper, depend ng on nd v dua c rcumstances. Comments concern ng the accuracy of th s t me est mate and suggest ons for reduc ng the burden assoc ated w th the t me spent co ect ng th s nformat on shou d be d rected to the F nanc a Management Serv ce, Fac t es Management D v s on, Property & Supp y Sect on, 3361 -L 75th Avenue, Landover, MD. 20785 and the Office of Management and Budget, Paperwork Reduct on Project (1510-0043), Wash ngton, D.C. 20503. THIS ADDRESS SHOULD ONLY BE USED FOR COMMENTS AND/OR SUGGESTIONS CONCERNING THE AMOUNT OF TIME SPENT TO COLLECT THIS DATA. DO NOT SEND THE COMPLETED PAPERWORK TO THE ADDRESS ABOVE FOR PROCESSING.

Table 3-B How to Respond to the Notice of Reclamation

Steps to take Under Limited Liability

1. Immediately determine the account balance amount. Check for other types of Federal benefit payments that the deceased may have been receiving, if enough funds are available in the payee's account to satisfy the reclamation, the funds should be returned promptly through the Automated Clearing House (ACH) system within 60 days of the Notice (by doing so, the RDFI will obtain an immediate credit and prevent any further action). When returning the full amount of the Reclamation, the RDFI does not need to complete and return the FMS-133 to the Disbursing Office.

2. If funds are available, but not sufficient to satisfy the full reclamation, a partial payment should be remitted to the Government Disbursing Office that issued the reclamation. When returning less than the full amount, the RDFI should remit a check and attach the front and back copy of the Notice of Reclamation indicating on the reverse the total amount of the partial payment.

3. If Federal benefit payments are credited after an RDFI receives a reclamation. The RDFI should reply to the reclamation by returning the items listed on the notice (not to exceed the outstanding total) as well as any deposits received after receipt of the Notice of Reclamation.

4. Promptly mail the Notice to Account Owners* (Part 5) to the last known address(es) of the account owner(s) and notify the account owner(s) of any action that the RDFI has taken or plans to take against the account.

5. When the RDFI is returning less than the outstanding total listed on the Notice of Reclamation, the RDFI must complete and sign Certification No. 1*** and if the RDFI had no knowledge of the death at the time the payment(s) was received or withdrawn, also sign Certification No. 2**** on the back of the Disbursing Office copy of the Notice of Reclamation. There is no need to sign multiple pages or copies of the same form. The RDFI must provide name, address and phone number of persons who withdrew from the account or if it is a sole owner account the RDFI MUST provide the name, address and phone number on file for the deceased recipient. Return an amount equal to the account balance.

6. If the outstanding total** was previously repaid to the Federal government. The RDFI's obligation to the Federal government (e.g., by the beneficiary's survivor) has been satisfied and the RDFI must return the Notice of Reclamation, attaching proof of the repayment, so that it is received by the Government Disbursing Office within 60 days of the date on the Notice. (See Types of Evidence).

7. The signature in Certification No. 1*** and 2**** must be in black or dark blue ink. No other ink colors, pencil, rubber-stamped, or other reproduced signatures will be accepted. The original signature must include at least the signer's first initial and last name. The signer's title and the date signed (in the signature block) may be rubber-stamped or reproduced. If the Notice of Reclamation is incorrect due to error in fact or date of death, (see Learning of an Error).

8. When returning the Notice of Reclamation, or sending correspondence to the government about the reclamation, the RDFI must use the address of the Government Disbursing Office found at the top right corner of the reclamation. Replying to any other address may delay the process and put the RDFI at risk of not responding with the 60 day deadline.

---

*   Some withdrawers may wish to restore all or part of the withdrawn post-death payments to the account upon receipt of a Notice of Reclamation to Account Owners. Repayment to the account by the withdrawer upon receipt of the Notice of Reclamation is not required or requested by the government.

**   The Outstanding Total is the sum of all Federal benefit payments received after death or legal incapacity, minus any amount returned to or recovered by the government.

***   Certification No. 1 on the back of the Disbursing Office copy of the Notice of Reclamation certifies that: the Notice to Account Owners was sent; account owners were notified of any action the RDFI has taken or plans to take against the account; and the RDFI took proper corrective action regarding any error in date of or fact of death.

****   Certification No. 2 on the back of the Disbursing Office copy of the Notice of Reclamation, certifies that the RDFI had no actual or constructive knowledge of the death at the time of deposit or withdrawal of any of the post-death payments; and, that the RDFI has returned the amount of the account balance to the government.

Incomplete or Inadequate RDFI Replies

If the RDFI's response is incomplete or inadequate, the government will send the RDFI a rejection letter **only one time**, clearly indicating what is lacking. If the RDFI's subsequent reply is still incomplete or inadequate, the government will initiate a debit action for the outstanding amount. Also, if an inadequate reclamation reply is received by the government two (2) business days or less before the Reclamation's deadline, the government will not reject it, due to lack of time. Instead, the government will initiate a debit action for the outstanding amount

Time Limits for Federal Reclamations

1. **INITIATION OF RECLAMATION (120-Day Protest):** The authorizing Federal agency must initiate the reclamation within 120 calendar days after the date that the agency first has actual or constructive knowledge of the death or legal incapacity of a recipient or the death of a beneficiary.

   An RDFI has the right to protest a Notice of Reclamation if it believes the agency did not meet the deadline for initiating the reclamation. The protest letter should be sent to the Disbursing Office and must include the claim number, RDFI contact person, a brief explanation, and any information/ documentation that supports the claim. It is strongly recommended that the RDFI send the completed FMS-133 along with the protest letter. By providing the completed FMS-133, the RDFI will be in the best position to limit its liability in the event the protest is denied. The FMS-133 should include the name and last known address and phone number of the following person(s):

   (A) The recipient and co-owner(s) of the recipient's account;

   (B) All other person(s) authorized to withdraw funds from the recipient's account; and

   (C) All person(s) who withdrew funds from the recipient's account after the death or legal incapacity of the recipient or death of the beneficiary.

   Upon receipt of the protest letter, the Disbursing Office will work with the authorizing Federal agency to determine whether or not the agency met the 120 day deadline. If the RDFI's protest is valid then the RDFI will be notified and the reclamation action will be withdrawn. If the protest is denied, and the RDFI qualifies for limited liability, the Disbursing Office will notify the RDFI and the RDFI will only be debited for the 45-day amount. If the protest is denied, **and the RDFI does not respond to the FMS-133**, the Disbursing Office will notify the financial institution and the agency may submit a request to debit the RDFIs Federal Reserve account for the full amount of the reclamation.

2. **SCOPE OF RECLAMATION:** An RDFI is not liable for any post-death benefit payments made more than six years prior to the date of the notice of reclamation, except under the following circumstance: "If the account balance at the time the RDFI receives the notice of reclamation exceeds the total amount of all post-death or post-incapacity payments made by the agency during such six-year period, this limitation shall not apply and the RDFI shall be liable for the total amount of all payments made, up to the amount in the account at the time the RDFI receives the Notice of Reclamation and has had a reasonable opportunity (not to exceed one business day) to act on the notice." [31 CFR Part 210.10(d)]

3. **COINCIDING WITH DATE OF DEATH:** An RDFI is not liable for any benefit payment dated (whose effective date is) the same as the date of death.

4. **RDFI REACTION TIME:** The RDFI, upon receipt of the government's Notice of reclamation, has UP TO ONE BUSINESS DAY to react to that reclamation by determining the account balance, and by preventing any further withdrawals of post-death government benefit payments from the account, if possible under the terms of the contract with the account holder.

5. **RDFI RESPONSE DEADLINE:** The RDFI has up to 60 days from the issue date of the reclamation to provide a full and accurate response to the proper Government Disbursing Office. Failure to respond timely may result in a debit to the RDFI's Federal Reserve account or the account of its correspondent for the total amount of the reclamation. This debit action will be final.

Follow-up to the Notice of Reclamation (FMS-2942)

A Follow-Up Notice is sent if the Government Disbursing Office does not receive a response within 30 days of the FMS-133, Notice of Reclamation; or if the RDFI's response to the Notice of Reclamation was incomplete or inaccurate.

A Follow-Up Notice is a reminder to the RDFI that a response to the Notice of Reclamation (FMS 133) must be received by the Government Disbursing Office within 30 days or the RDFI will forfeit the right to limit its liability.

A copy of the original Notice of Reclamation is attached to the Follow-Up Notice.
Any questions regarding this matter should be directed to the Government Disbursing Office shown in the upper right corner of the Notice of Reclamation.

Note: If the Reclamation deadline is imminent, the RDFI should consider using overnight mail or some similar means to be sure to meet the government's deadline. If the RDFI wants proof it met the deadline, it should consider using certified "return receipt" mail or similar means for a signed receipt.

Sample FMS-2942, Follow-up Notice

DIRECT DEPOSIT

**ELECTRONIC FUNDS TRANSFER
FEDERAL RECURRING PAYMENTS**

**FOLLOW-UP TO
NOTICE OF RECLAMATION**

FROM:

DATE:

REFERENCE: NOTICE OF RECLAMATION DATED: _____ (Copy Attached)

FOR: _____

(Name)   (Claim Number)

Your financial institution did not properly respond to the attached Notice of Reclamation as required by 31 CFR Part 210. In order to avoid the possibility of a debit to your Federal Reserve account or the account of your correspondent, a properly completed Notice of Reclamation must be received by this office within 30 days from the date of this notice.

ROUTING NUMBER:

TO: DIRECT DEPOSIT COORDINATOR

DEPARTMENT OF THE TREASURY
FINANCIAL MANAGEMENT SERVICE
PROGRAM MANAGEMENT DIVISION
FMS 2942 (3-89) EDITION OF 12-84 IS OBSOLETE

FINANCIAL ORGANIZATION COPY

Federal Agency Collection from Withdrawers

If all or part of the post-death payments have been withdrawn from the account before the RDFI learns of the death, and the RDFI properly responds to the Reclamation and is qualified to limit its liability, then the Reclamation process will be temporarily suspended and the authorizing Federal agency will attempt to collect the outstanding total from the withdrawer(s).

If the authorizing Federal agency is unsuccessful in collecting the outstanding total from the withdrawer(s), the RDFI or its correspondent's Federal Reserve account will be debited (for the 45-day amount) not to exceed the outstanding total.

Debit of the RDFI's Account

If the RDFI fails to respond completely and accurately to a Notice of Reclamation by the due date, the Government Disbursing Office will debit the RDFI's Federal Reserve account or that of its correspondent account for the full amount of its outstanding liability. This action is final.

If the RDFI responds correctly and accurately to a Notice of Reclamation by the due date, and the Federal agency is unable to collect the balance on the FMS-133, the RDFI will be debited for the 45 day limited liability amount.

The table below shows when the authorizing Federal agency can exercise its authority to have an RDFI's Federal Reserve account debited.

<u>Table 3-C</u>

If the RDFI:	Then the RDFI (or its correspondent's) Federal Reserve Account
Fails to respond accurately and completely to the Notice of Reclamation.	will be debited for the outstanding total.
Fails to respond within the 60-day time limit of the Notice of Reclamation.	
Responds accurately, completely, and timely, (i.e., limited its liability) but the authorizing Federal agency can no longer collect the outstanding total from the withdrawers.	will be debited for the 45-day amount not to exceed the outstanding total.

How to Identify Debits using the Reclamation Ticket Number

When there is a liability for an ACH reclamation payment by a receiving depository financial institution (RDFI), the RDFI will receive a charge to their Federal Reserve Account. The reclamation ticket number will appear on the FIs Statement of Account. This ticket number is the same number as identified on the original FMS-133, Notice of Reclamation.

The FMS-133, Notice of Reclamation form provides the reclamation ticket number in the top right box of the form to the right of the date. It is important that you retain a copy of the original reclamation notice until the associated case is closed. All financial institutions should be capturing and storing the reclamation ticket number with the reclamation information. This ticket number should be used to identify debits for reclamations. **Coordination between the ACH reclamation area and your accounting department is critical to the reconcilement of your Statement of Account.**

Provided below is an example of how the debit for ACH reclamations will appear on your FRB Statement of Account:

```
                                                       Reclamation
                                                       Ticket Number

9914 (510) 594-7183 57210 Treas ACH Rec Auto
BR      BATCH REF   OFFSET FI                  DEBIT
        03884 7502  051000033 21234456         500.00
```

Explanation of the Debit:

1) 9914 indicates an entry processed by FRB Philadelphia to an out of district bank.

2) This is the phone number of the RFC that initiated the debit. It is also provided in the upper right hand corner of the reclamation notice.

3) 57210 is the transaction code representing an automated debit on ACH reclamations from the San Francisco RFC. This transaction code number will be unique for each RFC. (See Table 3-D)

4) 03884 represents a batch number.

5) 7502 represents a reference number.

6) 051000033 is the FRB Philadelphia routing number.

7) 21234456 is the Reclamation Ticket number. This will be unique for each reclamation and is the same number as assigned on the original Notice of Reclamation, (FMS-133) form.

8) The dollar amount of the debit is indicated in the far right hand column.

Table 3-D

Transaction Codes for ACH Reclamations

The table below shows the unique transaction codes numbers for each Regional Financial Center.

Transaction Code	Transaction Code Description	Definition	Daylight Overdraft Posting Times
57170	Treas ACH REC Auto	Debits for reclamation payments authorized by the Treasury to post to a financial Institution. These payments are initiated to FRB Philadelphia by the **Kansas City Regional Financial Center** Includes adjustments to such entries.	After close of Fedwire
57190	Treas ACH REC Auto	Debits for reclamation payments authorized by the Treasury to post to a financial Institution. These payments are initiated to FRB Philadelphia by the **Philadelphia Regional Financial Center** Includes adjustments to such entries.	After close of Fedwire
57210	Treas ACH REC Auto	Debits for reclamation payments authorized by the Treasury to post to a financial Institution. These payments are initiated to FRB Philadelphia by the **San Francisco Regional Financial Center** Includes adjustments to such entries.	After close of Fedwire

C. Errors in Death

If the Person did not Die

If the RDFI obtains satisfactory proof that the recipient or beneficiary is alive, the RDFI is still required to complete and return the Notice of Reclamation (see Table 3-E Step Action). Failure to respond to the Notice of Reclamation will result in a debit to the RDFI or its correspondent's Federal Reserve account for the outstanding total. In this case, a debit can only be restored after a verification process by the authorizing Federal agency.

Types of Evidence

The following are acceptable types of proof for verifying that the person did not die:

- Driver's license, picture ID or other evidence similar to that required for cashing a check, if the recipient or beneficiary appears at the RDFI.

- A signed, dated, and notarized statement attesting to the fact that the recipient or beneficiary is alive if, he/she is unable to appear at the RDFI.

- A written statement from the authorizing Federal agency verifying that the recipient or beneficiary is alive.

The RDFI is not obligated to accept the proof or to contact the authorizing Federal agency if any disagreements or questions arise with the person presenting the proof. Prudence is required, as the action taken by the RDFI may affect its liability. Disagreements will be adjudicated by the authorizing Federal agency after it has been contacted by the person presenting the proof.

Accepting the Proof

The table below shows what actions the RDFI must take if it accepts the proof that the person did not die.

Table 3-E

Step	Action
1.	Correct the error in the fact of death on the Disbursing Office Copy of the Notice of Reclamation.
2.	Sign Certification #1 on the back of the Disbursing Office Copy of the Reclamation, certifying that a correction has been made.
3.	Timely return the Notice of Reclamation with a copy of proof of error in fact of death to the Government Disbursing Office.
4.	Advise the recipient to contact the authorizing Federal agency to restart payments.

Rejecting the Proof

The table below shows the actions the RDFI must take if it rejects the proof that the person did not die.

Table 3-F

Step	Action
1.	Continue to process the Notice of Reclamation, which includes sending the Notice of Reclamation to account owner(s).
2.	Refer the person presenting the proof to the Federal agency.
3.	Notify the account owner(s) to provide a written statement from the Federal agency verifying that the recipient or beneficiary is alive, or the reclamation process will continue.

Restarting Payments

Once a reclamation has been processed, all further benefit payments will be stopped. Presenting acceptable proof that the death report was in error (and stopping the reclamation process) does not restart the monthly benefit payments. The recipient or beneficiary must contact the authorizing Federal agency to re-enroll in Direct Deposit.

If the Date of Death is Wrong

The RDFI is authorized to adjust the outstanding total, provided it obtains acceptable proof that the date of death shown on the Notice of Reclamation is wrong. *When correcting a date of death error, the RDFI should always return the completed reclamation within the 60 day time limit in order to prevent the debit action.*

Day of the Month is Wrong

The table below shows the actions the RDFI needs to take if the day of the month is wrong.

Table 3-G

IF	THEN	AND
the day of the month of death is wrong	The RDFI must provide in its response a copy of the death certificate with the correct date of death because this could affect the calculation of the limited liability amount.	The RDFI must respond within 60 days to the Notice of Reclamation.
	Note: RDFI's are NOT authorized to make adjustments to the outstanding total if there is only an error in the day of death	

Month or Year is Wrong

The table below shows the actions the RDFI must take if the month or the year is wrong.

<u>Table 3-H</u>

Step	Action
1.	Enter the correct date of death on the back of the Disbursing Office Copy of the Notice of Reclamation.
2.	IF the correct date of death is

	• Later than the reported date of death	THEN go to Step 3.
	• Earlier than the reported date of death	the RDFI must...
		inform the account owners of the error; and check the appropriate box on the back of the Disbursing Office Copy of the Notice of Reclamation; and pay the amount listed on the Notice of Reclamation.
		Note: Additional payments will be collected by a subsequent reclamation. However, if the RDFI is aware of any additional post-death benefit payments, it is in its best interest to return them immediately.

Step	Action
3.	Sign Certification #1 on the back of the Disbursing Office Copy of the Notice of Reclamation.
4.	Complete the worksheet for adjusting the outstanding total. Refer to page 5-26
5.	Pay the appropriate amount using the adjusted outstanding total. If the amount returned is less than the adjusted outstanding total... • sign Certification #2 on the back of the Disbursing Office Copy of the Notice of Reclamation; and • provide name, last known address and phone number for all withdrawers, co-owners, and authorized signers.
6.	Return the completed Notice of Reclamation so it is received by the Government Disbursing Office within 60 days of the date on the Notice.

Learning of an Error After Completing a Reclamation

If the RDFI learns of an error in the date of death after returning a completed Notice of Reclamation and it has already satisfied its liability, it MUST contact the authorizing Federal agency (based on the payment type listed on the Notice of Reclamation) to make the appropriate adjustment.

If the RDFI is due a refund, the RDFI must provide supporting documentation to the authorizing Federal agency.

 Note: Only the authorizing Federal agency can make adjustments after the debit action has been processed.

Worksheet for Adjusting the Outstanding Total if the Date of Death is Wrong

The worksheet below may be used by the RDFI to calculate the adjusted total if there is an error in the date of death.

Table 3-I

	PMT 1	PMT 2	PMT 3	PMT 4
List the month/day/year of each payment shown on the Reclamation form.	____	____	____	____
For each payment (shown on the Reclamation) did the person die before the date of the payment? (Enter "yes" or "no")	____	____	____	____
For each "yes", enter the dollar amount of the payment. (Do not enter the dollar amount if "no.")	____	____	____	____
Total all "yes" payments $_____ (This is the adjusted outstanding total to use on the Notice of Reclamation).				

D. Subsequent Notice of Reclamation

The government may issue a subsequent Notice of Reclamation if the original Notice of Reclamation did not list all post-death benefit payments.

A subsequent Reclamation <u>will</u> be issued if the following apply; the date of death was earlier than shown on the original Notice of Reclamation, account number changed, and/or routing number changed.

What to do

The table below shows what actions the RDFI must take if it receives a subsequent reclamation:

Table 3-J

Step	Action
1.	Respond as it would to an original Notice of Reclamation (See Table 3-B).
2.	Attach a brief cover letter, indicating that this is a subsequent Notice of Reclamation.

Previous debit

If the RDFI has already limited its liability and has been debited for the 45-day amount on the original reclamation case, it will not be debited again on a subsequent Reclamation for the same case. However, in order to maintain its limited liability status the RDFI must respond to all Notice of Reclamations received to prevent a debit to the RDFI or its correspondent's Federal Reserve account.

E. Contacts

FMS Payment Management Call Center　　　　(855) 868-0151

6 Federal Government Notification of Change

Overview

Notification of Change (NOC) is used to change and/or correct account information for Federal government transactions processed through the Automated Clearing House (ACH). Although the Federal government basically follows NACHA Operating Rules for NOCs, some of the data requirements for Federal government NOCs are not the same as those for commercial NOCs. The procedures contained in this chapter apply only to Federal government NOCs.

In this Chapter...

A: Introduction to Notification of Change

Notification of Change (NOC) is a method used by a financial institution to notify a Federal agency to correct or change account information in an entry the Federal agency processed through the ACH. Refer to NACHA Operating Rules for formats and instructions.

Note: *ENRs should not be used in place of NOCs to correct account information, unless the recipient is initiating a new Direct Deposit authorization or changing financial institutions.*

When to use NOCs

NOCs are used for Federal government (both civil and military) payments that are made on a recurring basis. Examples are:

Benefit Payments

- Department of Veterans Affairs
- Office of Personnel Management
- Railroad Retirement Board
- Social Security Administration
- Supplemental Security Income

Other Payment Types

- Federal salary
- *TreasuryDirect*
- Vendor and miscellaneous

When NOT to use NOCs

To change	Recipient must
Title/ownership of account	
Interest of the recipient or beneficiary in the account	
From one financial institution to another	Complete a new enrollment (ENR)
Account information for one-time payments (e.g., IRS Electronic Tax Refunds)	
Name of recipient (e.g. following marriage)	. . . Contact the Federal agency that authorized the payment

Processing Timeframes

Generally, NOCs will be processed for the next ACH transaction. (Due to operational limitations, it may take two payment cycles for some NOCs to be processed.

What to do if an agency does not respond to an NOC within two payment cycles.

- Verify that the NOC was properly formatted. Make sure that the NOC contained the correct original RDFI routing number.

- If the NOC was correctly formatted, contact your FMS Regional Finance Center (RFC). See Contact information below. The RFC will work with the agency for resolution.

- Make sure that rejected NOCs are acknowledged and resolved (See below)

If you have any questions, contact

      The Payment Management Call Center, at 855-868-0151, Option 1.

Change Reason Codes

The Federal government's disbursing systems are only able to process the following six authorized NOC/Change codes: C01, C02, C03, C05, C06, and C07. The Federal agencies will not process any others.

The following table shows when to use the Change Reason Codes.

Change Reason Code	Change Reason	When to Use
C01	Incorrect Account Number	Correct data entry errors in the account information.
		Issue a new number to an existing account.
		Modify the account numbering system (e.g. to drop a branch code)
C02	Incorrect Routing Number (RTN)	Accommodate a merger or system consolidation.
		Change the RTN to the preferred RTN for the financial institution.

continued next page >

When to use Change Reason Codes (continued)

Change Reason Code	Change Reason	When to Use
C03	Incorrect RTN and Incorrect Account Number	Accommodate a merger or system consolidation.
C05	Incorrect Transaction Code	Change from checking to savings or savings to checking.
C06	Incorrect Account Number and Incorrect Transaction Code	Correct a data entry error in the account information, and change from checking to savings or savings to checking. Issue a new account number and transaction code.
C07	Incorrect RTN, Incorrect Account Number and Incorrect Transaction Code	Accommodate a merger or system consolidation.

Note: The only Transaction Codes recognized by the Federal government for NOCs are:

For checking (demand)	**For savings**	**For General Ledger**
22 (credit)	32 (credit)	42 (credit
27 (debit)	37 (debit)	

Claim Number Structure

Federal agencies have special structures for their claim numbers (Individual ID number). The claim number is important to identifying the payment recipient whose payment information must be changed.

Accurate formatting of the claim number is critical for processing changes. Note that pattern differences exist between Federal agencies. These claim numbers must include all spaces, hyphens, prefixes, suffixes, alphanumeric characters, and trailing or leading zeros that accompanied the original payment information.

Claim Number Structure Table

The following table represents correct claim number structures used in formatting NOCs.

Agency	Claim Number Structure	Example
Social Security Administration	999999999XX 999999999X 999999999	123456789C1 123456789A 123456789
Office of Personnel Management	Xb9999999bXb Xb9999999b9b	F_1234567_W_ A_1234567_0_
Department of Veterans Affairs	999999999b99b99 99999999b99b99	162306890_10_01 12345678_00_06
Railroad Retirement Board Retirement/Annuity	XXX999999999b9b Xbb999999bbbb9b XXbZZZZZ9bbbb9b	WCA123456789_7_ A__123456____1_ WD_000006____8_
Unemployment/Sickness	bbb999999999	___123456789
Department of Labor	999999999XXbXXb	123456789LW_MB_

Key: X = alphanumeric,   9 = numeric,   b = blank,   Z = zero filled,   _ = space

B: Other Change Methods

Financial institutions not using NOCs may continue to submit:

- corrected Direct Deposit Sign-Up Forms (SF 1199As) to Federal agencies, or
- letters to Federal agencies requesting changes

Financial Institution Actions

The table below contains instructions for financial institutions not using NOCs.

Type of Payment	Fewer than 100 payments, SUBMIT corrected photocopies of SF119As or letters to:	More than 100 payments CONTACT

Air Force
   Active Duty Reserve
   Air National Guard
	Defense Finance and Accounting Service Building 444/JMS	(303) 676-4326

Active Duty Allotments	6760 E. Irvington Place Denver, CO 80279-3000	(303) 676-7213

Army
   Active Duty Reserve
   Active Duty Allotments
	DFAS - Indianapolis Center 8899 E. 56th Street Indianapolis, IN 46249-2801	(888) 332-7411

Instructions for financial institutions not using NOCs (continued)

Type of Payment	Fewer than 100 payments, SUBMIT corrected photocopies of SF119As or letters to:	More than 100 payments CONTACT
Bureau of the Fiscal Service Federal Housing Administration Debenture Payments	Bureau of the Fiscal Service Special Investments Branch P.O. Box 396 Parkersburg, WV 26106-0396	(304) 480-5299
TreasuryDirect	Bureau of the Fiscal Service Customer Assistance Branch P.O. Box 426 Parkersburg, WV 26102-0426 *Note: Financial institutions should submit systemwide changes to TreasuryDirect with the understanding that they agree to pay the Treasury and security owners for any losses resulting from errors made by the institution. (31 CFR Part 370.12)*	(800) 722-2678
Savings Bonds	Federal Reserve Bank of Pittsburgh P.O. Box 299 Pittsburgh, PA 15230-0299	(800) 322-1909
State and Local Government Series Securities Payments United States Mortgage Guaranty Insurance Company and Tax Loss Bonds Payments	Bureau of the Fiscal Service Special Investments Branch P.O. Box 396 Parkersburg, WV 26106-0396	(304) 480-5299

continued next page >

Instructions for financial institutions not using NOCs (continued)

Type of Payment	Fewer than 100 payments, SUBMIT corrected photocopies of SF119As or letters to:	More than 100 payments CONTACT
Coast Guard		
Active Duty	Commanding Officer (Code PS) US Coast Guard Pay and Personnel Center 444 SE Quincy Street Topeka, KS 66683-3591	(785) 339-3506
Reserves	Commanding Officer (Code RES) US Coast Guard Pay and Personnel Center 444 SE Quincy Street Topeka, KS 66683-3591	(785) 339-3506
Retired	Commanding Officer (Code RPD) US Coast Guard Pay and Personnel Center 444 SE Quincy Street Topeka, KS 66683-3591	(785) 339-3416
Department of Veterans Affairs		
Veterans Compensation, Pension or Education (MGIB)	VA Regional Office that maintains the veteran's records	(877) 838-2778
Veterans Life Insurance		(215) 842-2000 ext. 14270
Federal Salary and Allotment payments (including payments by the military to civilian employees) (FED SALARY)	Federal employing agency authorizing the payment (address where original SF 1199As were mailed). If address is unknown, contact recipient/member.	
Marine Corps Active Duty/Reserve Active Duty Allotment	DFAS - Kansas City Center 1500 E. 95th Street Kansas City, MO 64197-0001	(888) 332-7411

continued next page >

Instructions for financial institutions not using NOCs (continued)

Type of Payment	Fewer than 100 payments, SUBMIT corrected photocopies of SF119As or letters to:	More than 100 payments CONTACT
Navy Active Duty Reserve	DFAS - Cleveland Center/JFECA 1240 East Ninth Street Cleveland, OH 44199-2055	(216) 522-5855
Retirement Pay Army, Air Force, Navy and Marine Corps	DFAS - Cleveland Center Retired Pay Operations P.O. Box 99191 Cleveland, OH 44199-1126	(800) 321-1081 fax: (800) 469-6559 Washington, DC Metro area ONLY (202) 606-0500
Office of Personnel Management Civil Service Retirement (Annuity) (CIVIL SERVE)	Office of Personnel Management Retirement Operations Center P.O. Box 45 Boyers, PA 16017	(888) 767-6738 fax: (724) 794-6633
Railroad Retirement Board Railroad Retirement (RR RET)	Railroad Retirement Board Direct Deposit Coordinator 844 North Rush Street Chicago, IL 60611	(312) 751-4704

C: Refused Notification of Change

Refused Notification of Change is an automated method used by a Federal agency to notify the originating financial institution that the NOC information initiated cannot be processed.

Federal Agencies Using Refused NOCs

The Social Security Administration (SSA), the Railroad Retirement Board (RRB), and the Office of Personnel Management (OMB) are the only Federal agencies processing Refused NOCs at this time.

Processing Timeframes

NOCs that cannot be processed are usually refused to the financial institution before the next payment is submitted.

Refused NOC Codes

There are six refused NOC codes authorized for Federal government ACH entries: **C64, C65, C66, C67, C68. C69**.

The table below shows the refused NOC code and the reason why the original NOC was refused.

Code	Reason
C64	Incorrect individual identification
C65	Incorrectly formatted corrected data
C66	Incorrect discretionary data
C67	Routing Number not from original Entry Detail Record
C68	DFI Account Number not from original Entry Detail Record
C69	Incorrect Transaction Code

7 Contacts

Overview

This chapter includes addresses and/or phone numbers of ACH contacts. These contacts are provided to handle any problems or questions that you may have concerning ACH payments and collections.

In this Chapter...

A. FMS Regional Financial Centers (RFCs)

For assistance with a payment issued by Treasury (see DFAS section for contact information for payments issued by the Department of Defense), please contact the FMS Payment Management Call Center (855) 868-0151:

B. FMS ACH Liaison

For general ACH questions, please contact:

Treasury ACH Liaison... (202) 874-1251

C. EFTPS Assistance

If a taxpayer is initiating Federal tax payments using EFTPS—Through a Financial Institution (ACH Credit) see below for the appropriate customer service helplines.

Routing Number... 061036000
Account Number... 23401009
Taxpayer Enrollment/Helpline....................................... 1 (800) 555-4477 (Businesses)
                                                                  1 (800) 316-6541 (Individuals)
Financial Institution Helpline.. 1 (800) 605-9876

D. Major Paying Agency Contacts

Agency	Contact
Social Security Administration	1 (800) SSA-1213 or www.socialsecurity.gov
Office of Personnel Management	1 (888) 767-6738 or www.opm.gov/retire
Railroad Retirement Board	(312) 751-4704 or www.rrb.gov
Department of Veterans Affairs	1 (800) 827-1000 or www.va.gov
Veterans Compensation, Pension & Education	1 (800) 827-1000 or www.vba.va.gov/ro/muskogee
Veterans Life Insurance	1 (800) 669-8477 or www.insurance.va.gov
Bureau of the Fiscal Service	www.publicdebt.treas.gov
TreasuryDirect	1 (800) 943-6864 or www.treasurydirect.gov
Internal Revenue Service	1 (800) 829-1040 or www.irs.ustreas.gov
Department of Labor Black Lung	1 (800) 638-7072 or www.dol.gov/esa/regs/compliance/owcp/bltable.htm See also Chapter 1, Appendix 2
Federal Employee Workers' Compensation	See Chapter 1, Appendix 2, and/or www.dol.gov/esa/contacts/owcp/fecacont.htm
Longshore and Harbor Workers' Compensation	(202) 693-0925 For address, see Chapter 1, Appendix 2, or www.dol.gov/esa/owcp/dlhwc/lstable.htm

E. Defense Finance and Accounting Service (DFAS) Contacts

For information about military retirement and annuitant payments, please contact 1-800-321-1080. For additional information about payments disbursed by the military, please visit www.dfas.mil.

F. Go Direct Contact Information

For information about Go Direct, please contact 1 (800) 333-1795 (English) or 1 (800) 333-1792 (Spanish) or visit www.godirect.org.

8 Glossary

ACH Rules

The Operating Rules and the Operating Guidelines published by the National Automated Clearing House Association (NACHA), a national association of regional member clearing house associations, ACH Operators and participating financial institutions located in the United States.

Actual or Constructive Knowledge

When used in reference to an RDFI's knowledge of the death or legal incapacity of a recipient or death of a beneficiary; actual or constructive knowledge means that the RDFI received information, by whatever means, of the death or incapacity and has had a reasonable opportunity to act on such information or that the RDFI would have learned of the death or incapacity if it had followed commercially reasonable business practices.

Agency

Any department, agency, or instrumentality of the United States Government, or a corporation owned or controlled by the Government of the United States. The term agency does not include a Federal Reserve Bank.

Annuitant

A retired Federal employee or his/her survivor who is receiving payments from the Office of Personnel Management; a retired railroad employee, his/her spouse, or his/her survivor who is receiving payments from the Railroad Retirement Board; a retired military service person, his/her spouse or his/her survivor who is receiving payments from a military service.

Annuity

A recurring payment made to a retired individual, his/her survivor or spouse.

Automated Clearing House (ACH)

A funds transfer system governed by the NACHA Operating Rules which provides for the interbank clearing of electronic entries for participating financial institutions.

Automated Standard Application for Payments (ASAP)

A recipient-initialized payment and information system, designed to provide a single point of contact for the request and delivery of Federal funds.

Authorizing Agency

The Federal agency that authorized the initiation of the payment.

Banking Day

With reference to a financial institution, any day on which such financial institution is open to the public during any part of such day for carrying on substantially all of its banking functions, and, with reference to an ACH Operator, any day on which the appropriate facility of such ACH Operator is being operated

Beneficiary

A natural person who is entitled to receive all or part of a benefit payment. The beneficiary may or may not be the recipient.

Benefit Payment

A payment for a Federal entitlement program or for an annuity, including, but not limited to, payments for Social Security, Supplemental Security Income, Black Lung, Civil Service Retirement, Railroad Retirement annuity and Railroad Unemployment and Sickness benefits, Department of Veterans Affairs Compensation and Pension, and Worker's Compensation.

Business Day

A calendar day other than a Saturday, Sunday, or a Federal Holiday.

Cash Concentration or Disbursement (CCD)

A corporate ACH format consisting of one detailed payment record and one addenda record. The Fiscal Service primarily uses this format to process vendor payments.

CA$HLINK

A cash concentration and information system used to manage the collection of Federal government funds. It also provides agencies with financial information to verify bank deposits, ACH transfers, wire transfers, as well as information to reconcile their accounts.

Claim Number

A number which identifies the recipient's or beneficiary's records at the Federal agency that authorizes the payment; usually a Social Security Number or an equivalent identification number.

Claim Number Prefix

One or more alpha character(s) that precedes a claim number. These letters indicate the type of claim for which benefits are being paid.

Claim Number Suffix

A one or two alphanumeric character that follows the claim number. These characters indicate the type of claim for which benefits are being paid.

Corporate Trade Exchange (CTX)

A corporate ACH format consisting of one detailed payment record with up to 9,999 addenda records. The CTX format is used to transmit information in the ANSI X12 electronic data interchange (EDI) syntax.

Correspondent Bank

A bank that provides settlement with the Federal Reserve and/or processing services for another financial institution.

Customer Assistance Staff

A component of the Fiscal Service, Regional Financial Center that provides customer assistance to other government entities, the Federal Reserve Banks, financial institutions, and the public.

Death Notification Entry (DNE)

A notice to a Receiving Depository Financial Institution (RDFI) of the death of a Receiver. Only a Federal government agency may originate a DNE entry.

Direct Deposit

A Federal Government payment program for consumers who authorize the deposit of payments automatically into a checking or savings account via the ACH.

Direct Payment

An electronic transfer of funds authorized in advance by the remitter, permitting a Federal agency to collect payments automatically on a predetermined date. It is sometimes referred to as a preauthorized debit (PAD)

Discretionary Allotment

An amount permitted by the employing Federal agency to be deducted from a Federal government employee's net salary amount and paid to a recipient. The amount of discretionary allotments may not exceed the net pay due the employee for each pay period after all deductions required by law are subtracted.

Effective Entry Date

The date specified by the originator (authorizing agency) on which it intends a batch of entries to be settled. For credit entries, the effective entry date is one or two banking days following the processing date. For debit entries, the effective entry date is one banking day following the processing date.

Electronic Federal Tax Payment System (EFTPS)

A system through which taxpayers remit Federal tax payments electronically.

Enrollment (Automated) ENR

An ENR entry is a non-dollar entry sent through the ACH by any Receiving Depository Financial Institution (RDFI) to a Federal government agency participating in the ENR program for the purpose of transmitting Direct Deposit enrollment information. Sometimes referred to as Quick$tart™.

Electronic Transfer Account (ETA^{SM})

A low cost account designed by Treasury to provide individuals who receive Federal benefit, wage, salary, or retirement payments the ability to receive their payments electronically. Any individual who receives a Federal benefit, wage, salary or retirement payment is eligible to open an ETA.

ETA Provider

Financial institutions that choose to offer ETAs. They must enter into a Financial Agency Agreement with the Treasury Department.

FastStart

An abbreviated SF 119(A form used to enroll and/or make changes to Direct Deposit information.

Federal Payment

Any payment made by an agency. The term includes, but is not limited to:
(1) Federal wage, salary, and retirement payments; (2) vendor and expense
reimbursement payments; (3) benefit payments; and (4) miscellaneous payments
including, but not limited to, interagency payments; grants; loans; fees;
principal, interest, and other payments related to United States marketable and
nonmarketable securities, overpayment reimbursements; and payments under
Federal insurance or guarantee programs for loans.

Federal Reserve Bank

Serves as the nation's central bank and the Federal government's fiscal agent.
It processes electronic payments, including ACH, for the Federal government,
handling Federal government deposits and checks, and supervising and regulating
Federally chartered financial institutions.

Financial Agency Agreement

Agreement between Treasury and financial institutions who offer ETAs. Outlines the
duties of the financial institutions.

Financial Institution

A bank, savings bank, saving and loan association, credit union or similar
institution.

Flagging

The automated marker on an account indicating that one or more account holders
is deceased, and that all future Federal payments for that account should be
returned.

Financial Organization Master File (FOMF)

A master list of financial institutions receiving Federal government Automated
Clearing House (ACH) payments. It contains Routing Numbers (RTNs) and a single
financial institution name and mailing address for each RTN.

45-Day Amount

The dollar amount of all the ACH payments received within 45 calendar days
following the death or legal incapacity of a recipient or the death of a beneficiary.

Government Disbursing Office

A Federal government office which issues payments on behalf of an authorizing Federal agency.

Legal Incapacity

A legal declaration that an individual is unable to manage his/her affairs properly.

Limited Liability Amount

The sum of the account balance and the 45-day amount. The limited liability amount is the financial institution's liability for benefit payments if funds have been withdrawn from the account after the death and the financial institution meets all requirements for limiting its liability. This amount may not exceed the outstanding total.

Lockbox (paper)

A post office box established by a financial institution for the purpose of receiving paper-based payments to an agency.

Lockbox (electronic)

An account established buy a financial institution for the purpose of receiving ACH payments to an agency.

NACHA - The Electronic Payments Association

The trade association which sets automated payment standards that govern the ACH system for financial institutions nationwide.

Notice of Reclamation

A Notice sent by electronic, paper, or other means by the Federal government to an RDFI which identifies the benefit payments that should have been returned by the RDFI because of the death or legal incapacity of a recipient or death of a beneficiary.

Originating Depository Financial Institution (ODFI)

The financial institution which delivers ACH entries directly or indirectly through a third party to its ACH operator.

Outstanding Total

The sum of all benefit payments received by an RDFI from an agency after the death or legal incapacity of a recipient or the death of a beneficiary, minus any amount returned to, or recovered by, the Federal government.

Prearranged Payment and Deposit (PPD)

The ACH format used by the Federal government for consumer payments.

Preauthorized Debit (PAD)

See Direct Payment.

Quick$tart™

See Enrollment (Automated) ENR.

Reclamation

A procedure to recover Federal government recurring benefit payments that were paid through ACH after the death or legal incapacity of a recipient or the death of a beneficiary.

Receiving Depository Financial Institution (RDFI)

For the purposes of the Green Book, the RDFI is the financial institution that receives the payment.

Recipient

A natural person, corporation, or other public or private entity that is authorized to receive a Federal payment from an agency.

Regional Financial Center

The Fiscal Service regional centers that act as the Government Disbursing Office for Treasury disbursed payments.

Remittance Express (REX)

Remittance Express is a program designed to improve and streamline the process by which private sector remitters initiate payments (ACH credits) to the Federal government. REX allows a Federal agency to use the ACH network to receive payments from its remitters

Representative Payee

A person or institution authorized by an authorizing Federal agency to accept payments for the benefit of one or more other persons, such as legally incapacitated adults or dependent children.

Tele-TRACE

A research method where a Government Disbursing Office representative will contact a financial institution, *by telephone*, to resolve a payee's claim that he/she did not receive an ACH payment.

Trace Number

A fifteen-digit number assigned to identify each ACH item by the issuing Government Disbursing Office. The first eight digits are the Disbursing Office's routing number and the last seven digits are the trace item number. It is also part of the original payment data forwarded to the financial institution and is included in each Entry Detail, Corporate Entry Detail, and Entry Detail Addenda Record.

Trace Request (FMS 150.1 or FMS 150.2)

A form sent by the Government Disbursing Office to a financial institution reporting a nonreceipt claim by a payee for an ACH payment.

TreasuryDirect

TreasuryDirect is a book-entry securities system in which investors' accounts of book-entry Treasury marketable securities are maintained. It is designed for investors who purchase Treasury securities and intend to hold them until maturity.

Treasury Financial Manual

The manual issued by the Fiscal Service containing procedures to be observed by all agencies, Federal Reserve Banks, and financial institutions with respect to payments, collections, central accounting, financial reporting, and other government-wide fiscal responsibilities of the Treasury.

Third Party Processor

A company that receives and processes ACH transaction data for a financial institution.

Vendor Payment

The electronic transfer of funds and payment-related information used by the Federal government for payments to businesses that provide goods and services